THE CHURCH AND REVOLUTION

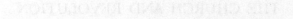

THE CHURCH AND REVOLUTION

Some reflections on the relationship of the Church to the modern world

by
REV. PETER J. RIGA

THE BRUCE PUBLISHING COMPANY / MILWAUKEE

NIHIL OBSTAT:

JOHN E. TWOMEY, S.T.L., PH.D.
Censor librorum

IMPRIMATUR:

✠ WILLIAM E. COUSINS
Archbishop of Milwaukee
July 24, 1967

For Patricia
"... with patience, upholding
each other in love. . . ."
Eph 4:2

Library of Congress Catalog Card Number: 67–28887

MADE IN THE UNITED STATES OF AMERICA

PREFACE

The Church and Revolution is an attempt to confront in a meaningful way the crucially important task facing the Church today: to proclaim the good news of Jesus to a world in ferment, in revolution. Never in recorded history have events moved with the pace they have during our lifetime. Today men stand on the threshold of a new era in human history. Advances won gradually, over a period of centuries in fact, for men of the western world must be communicated now to the developing and underdeveloped peoples of Africa, Latin America, and Asia. Throughout the whole world the "revolution of rising expectations" is in full swing, and the prospects offered to the human race by twentieth-century technological breakthroughs stagger the imagination. The age-old problems of war and peace, of human misery and poverty, of building the city of man remain; but the need to find the solution to these issues has only grown more urgent, more demanding. The Church must be in the vanguard of those working toward the alleviation of human misery and toward the construction of a world wherein the human community is leavened by the spirit of justice and love. The Church, as John XXIII and Vatican II have made eminently clear, must renew herself internally so that she can witness effectively to Christ *within* the world, incarnating among men the gospel of life and love.

Thus we have here focused attention, first, on the Church herself, and the revolutionary character of the movement inaugurated by John XXIII as he led the Church from the Constantinian era into a new age for the Church. There is crucial need to grasp the significance of what John and Vatican II have achieved in the matter of changing radically our *attitudes* toward the Church and toward the world. Vatican II proclaimed no new dogmas and in no way changed the substance of the faith handed on by the apostles and expressed in the great creeds of the early Councils or in the dogmatic constitutions of Trent. Yet John and Vatican II did change, and in a radical way, our way of viewing the Church, of looking upon the relationship of the Church to the world. And there can be no *aggiornamento* until this character of the Johannine revolution is grasped.

Next, it is important to set in focus the questions raised by twentieth-century capitalism and communism, for it is in confronting these issues that the Church fulfills her mission of worshiping God through service to men. Thus, two chapters explore the meaning of modern capitalism in the light of the Church's socioeconomic teaching and the challenge of Marxist atheism.

Third, we shall try to touch in more detail the precise relationship between Church and world, reflecting on the role of the layman within the Church as the Christian who is charged with making the gospel the leaven of the new humanism, witnessing to the saving Lord of history in the everyday world of temporal realities.

Finally, we shall explore the significance of Pope Paul's masterful encyclical on the development of peoples, linking this up to the theme of the Church of the poor.

St. Mary's College, California
July 28, 1967

CONTENTS

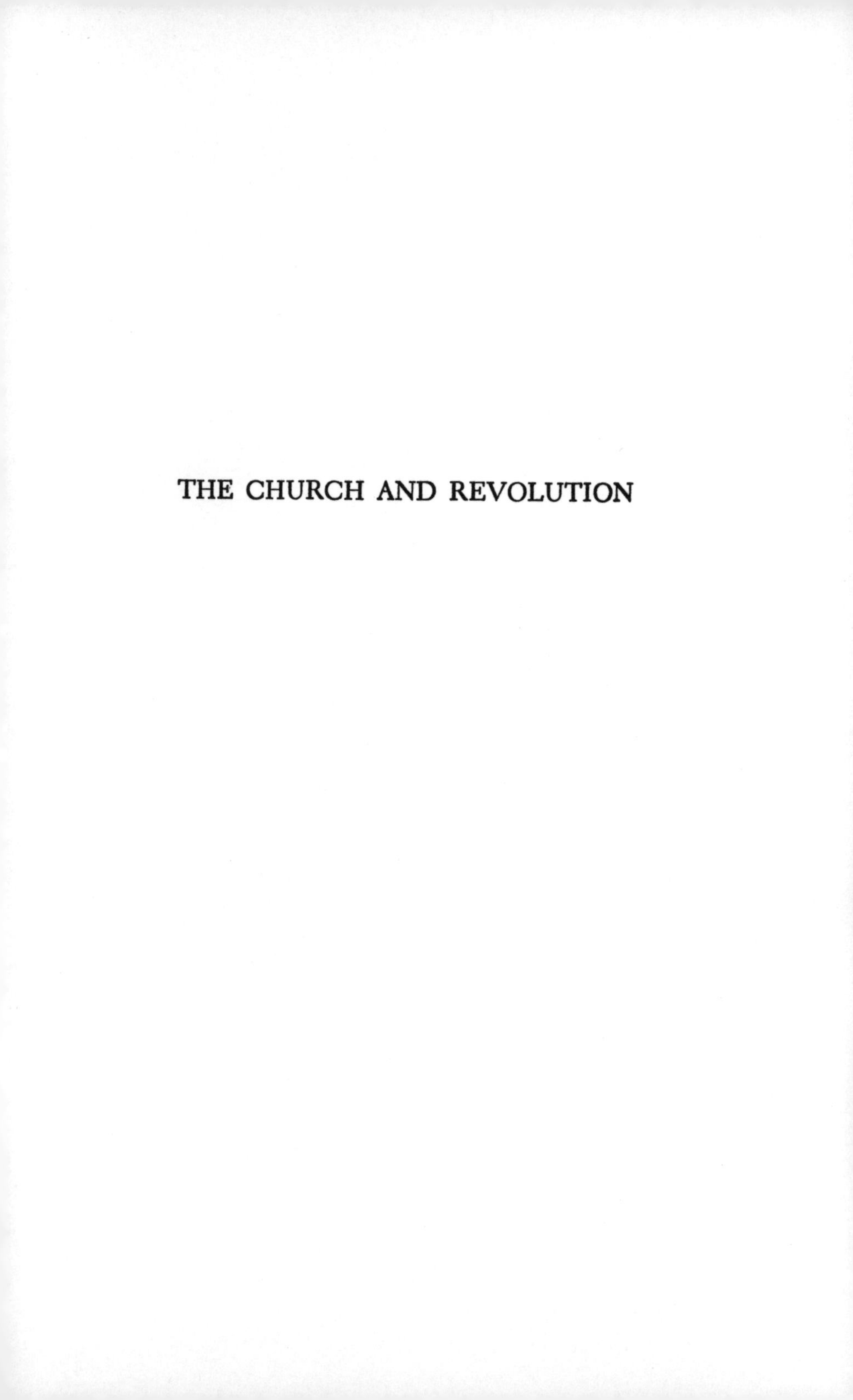

THE CHURCH AND REVOLUTION

CHAPTER I

REVOLUTION WITHIN THE CHURCH

I

The history of the Church can be roughly divided into three main divisions: (1) the age of "unestablishment" from the beginning to the year 312; (2) the age of establishment and limitation (the "Constantinian" era) from 312 to 1962; (3) the Johannine era, which has begun only an incredibly short time ago. Our object is to show that the Church has indeed moved into a new and decisive period of her history away from a reality which has been her living milieu for the past sixteen hundred years. Indeed, we hold that it is only to the degree that the Church discards much of the institutional, administrative, and cultural trappings of this immense period, that she will be able to understand and influence the contemporary world.

We speak of the first era of Church history as an "unestablishment" (disestablishment would not be a suitable term, since in this period the Church was a proscribed religion). It was a period of almost complete evangelical freedom from inhibiting cultural forms and from the paternalistic "protection" of civil authority. Many of the Church's early apologists and defenders of the faith endeavored to make the evangelical message meaningful in the context of the prevalent cultural patterns of the Roman Empire. The problem was not new. The Church had first to break with a stifling, Judaic, cultural pattern of ethnicity and particularism. The first crisis of the primitive Christian community centered on this problem, concretely exemplified in the relationship of the Mosaic Law to Christianity. Peter and Paul had it out in public when Paul rebuked Peter for his seemingly ambiguous attitude toward this problem. Thus Paul speaks of the freedom of the sons of God vis-à-vis every cultural particularism, even that of Judaism:

> But when Cephas came to Antioch, I opposed him to his face, because he stood condemned. For before certain men came from James, he ate with the Gentiles; but when they came he drew back and separated himself, fearing the circumcision party (Gal 2:11–12).

Emphasizing the fact that Christians are no longer subject to the cultural forms of a Jewish law (3:10–13), Paul concludes that the Word of God had made us free, subject no longer to ethnic, racial, or nationalistic accidentals:

> So, brethren, we are not children of a slave, but of a free woman in virtue of the freedom wherewith Christ has set us free; stand fast and do not submit again to a yoke of slavery (4:31–5:1).

The question was so serious and divisive that a Council of the Church had to be called to settle the matter (cf. Acts 15), and the principle was set down then and for all times to come: The Word of God is free of any particularizing constrictions: "For it has seemed good to the Holy Spirit and to us to lay upon you no greater burden than necessary things" (Acts 15:28). The early Church well at its beginnings had to make a break with a particular institution which threatened to constrict the freedom of God's word and the freedom of the Christian. This was and continues to be a momentous event for the Church. This decision of the apostolic Church incarnated the principle of a continuous *metanoia, aggiornamento,* or reform which will permit the Church for all time to be free of any particular sociological or cultural contexts, while allowing it the continuous freedom to seek out and incarnate itself in various cultures in order to achieve its mission of proclaiming Christ as Savior of mankind.

This, of course, was the guiding principle of the early Church for the first three hundred years of her existence. Her apologists attempted such a bridge and, with the exception of certain staunch eschatologists such as Tertullian, we witness during this period a successful attempt at dialogue with the Greco-Roman world. The successful adaptation of the gospel message to the culture of this world — an adaptation which in no way "watered down" the gospel — should serve the Church well as an example both for structuring her organization and for formulating the faith in terms intelligible to a particular culture. Even Tertullian talked more of eschatology and separation from the world than he practiced it. He did not hesitate to use Roman law and Greek philosophy to set forth and adapt the Christian message of salvation to the men of his day. Be that as it may, we have the illustrious examples of a Justin, Tatian, and Lactantius as well as many others. Here we have adaptation and incarnation of the Christian vision into the framework of Greco-Roman civilization. But this adaptation and incarnation were not "frozen," institutionalized, in these temporal structures. Freedom for further reformulations and structurings remained. It was only during the subsequent "Constantinian" era that the Christian faith became to some degree frozen in a given cultural framework.

II

With the Edict of Milan in 312 we have the beginnings of a new epoch, which is called today the Constantinian era. This lasted up to modern times. During this era theologians attempted, as did the early apologists, to put at the service of an incarnational Christianity a dynamism or *élan* which would help bring about as much as possible the terrestrial hopes implicit in the Word of God. During this era — spread over many centuries and incorporating within itself the Roman period, the Feudal period of the high and low Middle Ages, as well as post-reformation development — a whole complexus of institutional and juridical structures developed within the Church, and these structures, rooted in the legal, economic, and political culture of the Holy Roman Empire, would directly influence the spirituality of the Church as a whole. This Constantinian framework for ecclesial structures would eventually be the cause of untold sorrow for the Church in the modern world, from the time of the French and American revolutions to the present. During this period, and particularly during the period after Trent to the middle of the present century, the Church harks back to the past, refusing the freedom which was rightfully hers from the Word of God to extricate herself from a moribund culture and to become incarnate in the new culture of the modern age. Defensive rather than creative, she lost her opportunity to do so throughout the eighteenth, nineteenth, and early twentieth centuries by a list of *syllabi*, anathemas, and official *monita*. The *ancien régime* continued full force in the mentality or attitude of the Church throughout this period. One result was the Church's rejection of the new opportunities handed to her by an admittedly hostile modern world.

It is precisely this sad history and its consequences for the life of the Church in the world which is being shed today. Pope John, with his call for an *aggiornamento*, ushered in a new era for the Church, and the basic charter for the Church in the future was provided by Vatican II.

What we are speaking of here is beyond the question of doctrinal development, for no new or ancient dogmas are really involved. What is involved is a whole mentality, an outlook or spirit which has become institutionalized in the *status quo*, identifying a particularizing sociological expression of Christianity with the very concept of Christianity itself. Such an identification can only be disastrous, for culture is completely time-conditioned and as such requires continuous re-evaluation in the light of the ever new, ever renovating Word of God. This presupposes, of course, that it is agreed that some sort of incarnationalism of the Church in the world is a basic requirement of her being; or, in other words, that the relation of the Church to the world is not an extrinsic or ephemeral element of her constitution but rather an evidently implied command from her Divine Founder for every age of the Church's history. Thus something more than any particular dogma is concerned here, namely the whole pivotal point of the Church's efforts to bring salvation to men. She is, as the ancient Fathers of the Church used to say, the continuation of Christ: a continuous incarnation, following the law of the incarnation.[1]

This modern world is no longer that of the *ancien régime* or of the Middle Ages, with its stifling narrowness of view and firmly established cultural patterns particular to one small peninsula called Europe; it is rather a world of universal and cosmic dimensions and is in a constant state of flux and rapid change. The world today is no longer constricted or restricted by the "Christian civilization" of the West. It has long since cast aside the particularized ghetto mentality exemplified by Belloc's dictum that "Europe is the Faith." It is time that the Church and her members liberate themselves from this mental block. The continuation of this mentality among Christians is the reason for their fear and paranoid attitude toward this world of the twentieth century. We need not describe in detail the residue of the Constantinian age and the way it has been shattered by the revolutionary character of the modern world. Today we realize that unless the Christian man can dynamically re-orientate himself to this world and adapt to it, then, to use a favorite phrase of our day, God is indeed dead for modern man. If it is true that the Word became flesh, communicating thereby the effects of his divinity to the culture and world about him, then the Church can and must become incarnate within the temporal structures of men. Any other attitude is an evasion of her deep

[1] See the document on the Church (*Lumen Gentium*) of Vatican II, par. 1.

responsibility to and for the world and becomes the infidelity to her mission at this time of her incarnational existence.

This second era of the Church, then, has characterized and continues to characterize the mentality and approaches of the Church of our day. It is extremely important to analyze its roots and thus attempt to find a solution for our dilemma. Foremost during the Constantinian era and characteristic of the temporal incarnation of the Church in this period was the relationship of the temporal and spiritual powers. The close link between altar and throne when it was first brought into effect, clearly distinguished the Church from what it had been in the past, for during the beginnings the Church had been more or less antagonistic to the secular powers. With the edict of Milan, the Church became a recognized power in the worldly sense of that word (to exercise power here is to influence decisively the flux of human events), where she was respected and recognized in public law. The Emperor, however, remained the *Summus Pontifex* and retained this role by his consecration during the Middle Ages right up to the modern age when Napoleon is crowned Emperor by the Pope. In a sense, this consecration was a legitimization of the secular power to exercise its powers in "Christendom" — that particularized segment of the human family restricted to Europe. This resulted in the well-known reciprocal benefit theory: reciprocal defense, protection of one by the other. One consequence was that the Church did not possess the freedom which is hers by reason of the Word of God (judgment on all temporal structures). Instead of becoming incarnate within a culture, she became *identified* with a particularizing structure of a particular time. The gospel itself became a way of legitimizing a political regime; the sacral became profane and the profane participated in the sacral. Moral good became the object of both moral and public law, for the latter not only encouraged the former but also, by decree, helped to bring it about through the "secular arm of the state." The function of civil law was seen to consist in making Christian morality obligatory, so that the professional men of law throughout this period became experts in *utroque iure*. This had the inevitable result of prosecuting heresy on both religious and secular grounds as detrimental to the "common good" of a society in which the secular and the sacral were intimately intertwined.

This outlook continued into the Middle Ages, and as a result we have the Crusade ("Deus vult") against both infidels and heretics. Even the otherwise peaceful St. Augustine finally invoked the power of the state to stamp out and control the Donatists who were a danger to public order, a public order, however, in which the interests of both Church and state became effectively co-extensive. The ruler as ruler must submit to the gospel and if he failed to do so was to be treated as an outcast; his decrees must no longer be obeyed.

The inauspicious beginnings came when St. Ambrose of Milan refused the Emperor Theodosius admittance to the episcopal Church. The king or emperor was not just the defender of the common good but of the interests of the Church as well. Henry VIII of England was called the *Defensor Fidei* which, in a sense, could be said of all the secular rulers of this whole era. By his consecration or coronation as the temporal ruler — emperor, king, duke, etc. — he not only took legitimate possession of secular power, but also entered into a relationship with the Church. In order to foster the "common good" of an undivided Christendom, he became the "secular arm" of the Church, offering it defense, aid, protection, and mutual cooperation. This state of affairs was one of the main reasons why the Popes at the end of this era, Gregory XVI and Pius IX, so vigorously fought the new concepts of democracy and religious liberty. Their opposition cannot be fully explained — as is often maintained in Catholic circles — by the fact that these incipient movements were anticlerical and shot through with intolerance for the Church as the result of extreme liberal philosophy; this is true to a certain extent, but more profoundly, the Church had become so identified with a past age — the *ancien régime* of union between Church and State — that these Popes actually thought that in upholding the one they were upholding the other. This was a grave error in understanding the relationship of the Church to the temporal or secular society.

The *malaise* has continued to the present, for the Church has not as yet made its complete peace with the new age, since she exists more as something "parallel to" the world than incarnate within it. Thus she has separate, non-incarnated, educational systems, charity structures, etc. A type of ecclesiastical concordism is in effect here. The Church wishes to become incarnate in new forms and adaptations, yet she remains apart in presence and action so that she is really not incarnate within the world but is rather alongside and at a distance. Thus crisis follows crisis, as do anathemas and condemnations. This painful era of rejection and condemnation, we shall see later, was brought to an end, at least in principle, by John XXIII.

Consequently, throughout this period, whoever is outside the Church is outside the law as well. The ghetto to which the Jew was confined was decreed for him not only by a predominantly Christian community, but was physically enforced by the secular authority. The *Cathari* — heretics who denied the reality of matter and a visible Church — had to be militarily subdued by crusades since they were a threat to both Church and state. The infidel was simply outside the law of civilized society, and this was true both in Christian Europe and Moslem Africa. Both the Christian and Moslem worlds developed an almost identical syncretism and identity of secular and religious interests. The crusades became "holy" wars on both sides. The doctrine of the "divine right" of kings emerged, making sedition to the crown a crime both in civil and ecclesiastical law. The crime lives today in the Code of Canon Law of the Latin rite. The doctrine of the "sacred" right of private property also emerged during this period, a time by the way, when property belonged to the king (and his supporters, the barons) and to the Church. It would take the Church of our day some seventy years to develop a coherent doctrine of social teachings (Leo XIII, *Rerum Novarum*; John XXIII, *Mater et Magistra* and *Pacem in Terris*) concerning the social responsibility of private property. Such a doctrine is absent as doctrine from this entire period, because the lands were in the hands of the divinely appointed "father" in the person of the king and feudal baron — a paternalism of universal extension. Even the papal states were considered a natural right of the papacy, since the latter was conceived more in terms of temporal power than as the agency of evangelical service independent of all temporal power and influence. This synergism extended to the concept of prince bishops, and was reflected externally, in royal robes, rings and other trappings which still exist today. Happily the Church is now attempting to eliminate this in many ways. (It is noteworthy here to mention that the whole concept of episcopal-papal authority in Vatican II's *Constitution on the Church* is seen once again in the evangelical terms of service and love.) These trappings, of course, are only incidental and would be of no consequence to the modern Church were it not for the type of mentality they betray in those who, still today, are attached to them. The mentality harks back to another era, which has long since disappeared from the pages of human history and whose outstanding remnants are still to be found in the Church, holding them back from a complete and honest confrontation with the modern world.

One further result of this mind-set is that the faith becomes inextricably linked to a particular national culture, with the consequence that faith and nationalism become one and the same thing. This tragic situation endures today, as is evident if one recalls that in 1965 the Polish Bishops could calmly, in the name of God, proclaim disputed territories along the Oder-Neisse for Poland and her culture and faith. Modern nationalism owes much to this confusion of religious faith with love for one's homeland. Nationalism is a form of ancient tribalism where the stranger is the *hostis* or enemy. Evangelical Christianity has broken down the accidental differences of race, color, and tribe, where all are one in Christ and where the greatest dignity is to belong to the family and people of God. This is the ever new and ever revolutionizing concept of the Gospel. When Christianity becomes totally identified with a particularizing culture, it degenerates to a form of local tribalism (nationalism) at the cost of its catholicity.

This, of course, must be carefully distinguished from the incarnational mission of the Church to every culture. For the Church is sent to absorb and baptize the genius and values of a culture, but in this process, unless the Church keeps her evangelical freedom and catholicity, she is in danger of identification and absorption. When this happens she becomes a bulwark for the *status quo* and nationalistic sentiments incompatible with her universal mission. When the Church becomes identified with a given culture or race or nation, she loses her identity as a gift from God, as the inbreaking of God into human history. Thus, the Church must preserve her freedom, despite the transient gains that are hers when she becomes an agency of the state.

The baleful effects of this freezing of the Church into the cultural framework of Western Europe were reflected in the missionary life of the Church. If the earlier Middle Ages had been a failure from a missionary point of view (closed in, as was this period, on its own culture), the latter period was not much more successful. Missionary activity became more vast in scale (India, China, Japan, North and South America). Yet here too the identification of the Church with European culture made missionary activity more or less a complete failure in the Far East and half a success (because of Spanish-Portuguese colonialism) in the Latin part of America. Ricci and De Nobile (and later Father Lebbe) tried to adapt new cultural forms, language, philosophical forms, and even liturgical structures from the lands they visited in order to incarnate Christianity. Their efforts were directly counter to a narrow Romanism which finally put an end to their efforts in the Far East and quite possibly has inhibited Christianity there to this day. Vitoria and Las Casas attempted to do in Latin America what Ricci and De Nobile had done in the East. But their success was limited, as was that of the Jesuits in Uruguay before their order was suppressed.

It is quite possible that the suppression of Jesuit missionary activity in Latin America, an activity intent on a complete adaptation of Christianity to and for the Indians, marks a turning point in Latin Church history. Not even to this day has the Church overcome its stigma as a foreign import since it has been identified with the transported *ancien régime*. Today it is seen as the defender of the *status quo* against radical social and economic change. When the Church becomes identified with these ahistorical and regressive forces of another age, she loses her power to influence the revolutionary modern world for good.

This has happened more than once in the modern history of the Church. When it does, she can expect only persecution, as in fact happened in Mexico in 1910 and in Cuba after 1960. The same was true in Hungary where the Church confused her role in upholding the Feudal *status quo* of another age mainly because she, along with the ruling classes, owned over twenty percent of the lands of Hungary.

These inhibitants to Christianity and its expansive power can be traced to a juridical and narrow Romanism which deeply influenced missionary activity. According to this particularistic vision, the Church has full coercive power and rights. The Church is sublimated, if you will, into a type of terrestrial kingdom where everything is regulated by minutiae of law and procedure. The Roman notions of authority, law, *societas*, justice, and juridical person become absorbed into Church law. Ecclesial authority was regarded more as a power than as a service, and the "right" of the Church vis-à-vis the temporal order became a main preoccupation of the canonist and theologian throughout this period. The charismatic character and prophetic office of the Church were largely ignored by Roman ecclesiastical law so that they all but disappeared as a theological treatise except in the great scholastics (St. Bonaventure, St. Thomas) and were not seriously resurrected until modern times, in particular, in the *Constitution on the Church*.

Without accepting the gross exaggerations condemned by Pius XII in his encyclical *Humani Generis*, we can truthfully say with Congar that ecclesiology from the thirteenth century on was built like the second temple of the Jews, sword in hand. The sword was directed by the Church against infringements on her powers by the state. The struggle began as far back as Gregory VII over the issues connected with lay investiture. The result during the later scholastic period was that the Church was conceived essentially as a juridical *societas* with its own rights, in opposition or rather in contrast to the *societas Civilis.* For the first time in history the religious body, in this case the Church, began to formulate this separation and independence from secular power. Certainly, the notions were already in vogue as far back as St. Ambrose, and St. Augustine, and were reflected in the famous *duo sunt* formula of Pope Gelasius in 494. The real formulation of the Church as a juridical society, however, was left to the medieval canonists, with the resultant struggles between Church and state throughout the Middle Ages. Thus began the separation of the tract of ecclesiology from the other tracts of theology, to become one of polemical apologetics in the face of secular and civil encroachments. In later centuries we have the added difficulties of conciliarism and the exaggerated theories of Occam, Wyclif, and Huss on the "spiritual Church" in opposition to the external and hierarchical elements in the Church. These excesses led to further emphasis in ecclesiology on the external elements in the Church. If one wishes proof of this he may consult one of the greatest ecclesiologists of the fifteenth century, Turrecremata, and his famous *Summa De Ecclesia.* This treatise is divided into: (1) The Universal Church; (2) The Roman Church; (3) The Primacy of the Roman Pontiff; (4) Ecumenical Councils; (5) Schismatics and Heretics. It has not one word on the interior and spiritual element of the Church. The result, then, of this whole movement was an excessive emphasis on the hierarchical and external aspects of the Church. Even the titles of these first treatises *de Ecclesia* betray their one-sided emphasis.

The earlier errors of Huss and Wyclif, coupled with a need of true reform in the Church "in head and members" led to the revolt of the sixteenth century. Once again, for the reformers, the external is relegated not only to the secondary and nonessential but to sinfulness itself. Since then, Reformation ecclesiology has been dominated by polemics between the Church and the Reform. Abundant evidence of this can be found in such eminent ecclesiologists as Stapleton (1598) and Bellarmine (1621). After this period, ecclesiology takes on a strictly apologetical point of view in defense of hierarchy, clergy, sacraments, etc. — in short, the visible aspects of the Church. It became, in the words of Congar, a true "hierarchiology" instead of a total ecclesiology.

Starting in this same period, other errors arose which only served to harden the tendency: Gallicanism, Jansenism, Febronianism, Josephism, and finally, in England, Episcopalianism. All these errors had in common the denial of the Church in one aspect or another of her hierarchial structure or teaching authority. These could be combated only by emphasis on the Church as an independent society, with a divinely constituted hierarchy and teaching authority.

Thus the concept of the Church throughout the Constantinian era was much more juridical than charismatic or eschatological in character. This was expressed in the almost infinite number of mandates, rescripts, privileges, and dispensations needed to do almost anything in the Church. Such concepts as the "people of God," the "Mystical Body of Christ," "the fraternal community of brothers" all but disappeared from manuals of theology and preaching — particularly after the Reformation. Ironically, the man who in the nineteenth century was most responsible for a return to the Scriptures and the Fathers leading to the present-day renovation of ecclesiology in *Mystici Corporis* and *De Ecclesia* started his career as a canonist. It was in such a canonical context that J. A. Moehler first exposed the mystery of the Church to his students.

The development of Moehler's ecclesiology can be divided into three distinct periods. (1) His first concept of the Church emerged while he was teaching Canon Law. This was a juridical concept, in line with the canonical conception of the *societas inequalis*; to use his own expression, "the concept of the Church falls under the more general concept of society." (2) In the second period, marked by the composition of his *Einheit*, Moehler saw that this definition was too juridical, too formalistic. Through his detailed examination of the Church Fathers and early Christianity itself, he saw that this definition was at variance with that of the Fathers, since they conceived of the Church as "something one and real, with the Holy Spirit as its life principle transcending all human categories, a work of God, the continuation of Christ." We have already seen how this definition emphasized the interior element of the Holy Spirit. What is important, however, is that Moehler saw that the canonical and juridical definition of the Church of his earlier years had to be enlarged to include the interior, invisible element in the Church. (3) Moehler progressed further in his thought. By continued study of the Fathers and early Christianity, Moehler finally reached in his *Symbolik* the conception of the Church as the continuation of the Incarnation of the Son of God. The interior element, the mystical essence of the Church, is kept, but applied differently. Christ wished to be propagated through space and time by a divine-human organization: His representation to humanity through all ages was aided by the action of His own Spirit whose function is to lead to Christ. As Moehler put it:

> The eternal unity of the Father and the Son in love is the source of Christ's mission, of the authority and law which keep the Church alive and produce her unity.

III

Not all was black during the Constantinian era of the Church's history. Some of the doctrinal and institutional developments of the period had their advantages, and each must be understood in historical context. It is well known, for instance, that from the fall of the Roman Empire to the middle of the eighth century the Church was literally forced to take on the task of promoting civic order in the secular city, since the state had suffered a complete breakdown under the onslaught of the barbarians. St. Augustine tells us of his woes and fatiguing labors in judging both civil and ecclesiastical cases even in his day (425). Missionary activity during this period was characterized by a vitality and fresh evangelical methods of adapting the word of salvation to European culture. The monasteries acted as centers and custodians of learning and of intellectualism in an age of disorder and chaos.

One of the greatest gifts of this era—at least in its middle stages (eleventh and thirteenth centuries)—was the use of human reason in developing the implications of the Christian faith. The whole subject of the interrelation between faith and reason went through a distinct evolution throughout this period. There was a distinct change of attitude on the part of theologians as to the value of human intelligence.

Among the Greek Fathers, Clement of Alexandria (210) spoke of certain pagan philosophers as *sophoi* or "theologians." Yet, if this is so, it is because such philosophers as Plato received their wisdom concerning God from the prophets in particular and the Old Testament in general. Thus theology means simply the knowledge of divine things. He says this explicitly: "Philosophy . . . had a parcel of truth . . . of the theology of the externally existing Word." Clement was, however, too closely related to the pagan notion of theology as a philosophy, but we see here one of the first indications on the part of Christian theologians that there is a genuine value in applying reason in an effort to understand more adequately the meaning of Christian faith.

Origen also spoke of the "theologians" among the Greeks; thus theologians were, for him, those pagan authors who treated of religion. Yet he began to purify the notion of *theologia* from its pagan context. Theology, for him, was the true doctrine of God, and, more specially, the doctrine of Christ the Savior considered as truly God. To "theologize" is used exclusively to speak of God and Christ in order to recognize and profess him as God, just as the pagans were accustomed in doing with reference to the Emperor.

With Eusebius of Caesarea, the Christian meaning of "theology" was fully acquired. He called St. John the "theologian" because his Gospel is a discourse or word about God. He gives the word a properly Christian meaning. Thus theology is exclusively the knowledge of the true God which cannot be applied to any false god. This was an innovation proper to Eusebius himself and consecrates the term for further Christian usage.

Denis the pseudo-Areopagite (ca. 520) continued this same tradition, but with the nuance (rather common among the Greek Fathers) that theology designates holy Scripture and the inspired authors of Scripture. He also fashioned the famous expression of "mystical theology" and drew the classical distinction between "a hidden, mystical theology which was with God [and] the other 'theology' which is manifest, more known, philosophical, and demonstrative." His notion of "negative theology" which would be very popular with later mystics, was also quite famous.

But from this time forward, the use of the term theology to designate "the true doctrine of the true God" was accepted among the Greek Fathers. It took on various shades of meaning according to diverse difficulties and heresies which each of the early Greek Fathers was called upon to face. St. Athanasius, in combatting Trinitarian errors, employed the word *theologia* to designate the sacred doctrine concerning the Trinity. And it is to the Greek Fathers that we owe the classical distinction between "theology," i.e., doctrine on the divinity of the three persons in the Trinity, and "economy" (*oeconomia*), or the doctrine of the Word and His Incarnation.

Among the Latins, St. Augustine was the first to give this word a proper Christian meaning. Before him, we can find little to show this. St. Cyprian and St. Ambrose did not even mention it. The only time it was used by Christians was in polemical writings against the pagans, and here its meaning was pagan. St. Augustine took the word from the pagans; utilizing its etymological meaning, he employed the term against them as the *vera theologia* which only Christianity possesses. Over and above the pagan usage to describe the origins of the world (*theologia naturalis*), Augustine used the word as a faithful adherence to its object, God. Nevertheless, his theology was still inspired by Plato.

It was only Abelard who would fix this notion of "theology" in its purely Christian context as the Greek Fathers had already done before him. Abelard (1142) gave it a thoroughly Christian meaning as designating Christian teaching and Christian doctrine (*sacra pagina, sacra doctrina, divina pagina* (or) *lectio, sacra scriptura*). He expanded the notion, then, to the sum of Christian doctrine for which he now (and tradition after him) used the term "theology." Thus, we must wait until the twelfth to thirteenth century for the term to take on its full meaning as we know it today. This sense of the term was incorporated into the thought of the great scholastics of the thirteenth century, such as St. Thomas.

This whole elaboration of the use of human reason in the explication of sacred doctrine was one of the most monumental achievements of this period. Nor must we forget that the "liberalizing" of theology in a new age (when Aristotle re-entered the West) did not come about without a heavy price. St. Thomas himself was considered a wild-eyed radical-liberal for integrating the task of reason within the revealed *data*. His views merited for him a stay of some fifty years on the index of forbidden books at the great intellectual city of Paris. It was only after his canonization that the ban was lifted.

The task of relating reason to faith and vice versa was to evolve quite differently from what St. Thomas had in mind. In the later Middle Ages, the power to reason was so stressed that theologians tended to neglect other cognitive and non-cognitive values in the epistemological process. There developed a great stress on the "immutables" of the "essence" of man, law, society, etc., and a rationalization of life itself. The cultural heritage of Rome and Greece was put to good use by conciliar definitions (*homoousia, ousia, prosopon, sarkothenta,* etc.) and a whole theology was to be built around such concepts. Yet, this process began to degenerate in dry, rational analyses of the fourteenth and fifteenth centuries, when reason was separated from living experience and there was an end of the healthy evolution of all human thought structures. The dire effects of this rationalism are still with us in an "essential" concept of "natural law" which takes little note of the evolutionary experience of man's historicity.

Opposition to this rationalism was very clear in Luther's theological development. For him, neither Scripture nor the teaching of the Fathers has any other objective than to convert us to Christ and to put this crucified Christ into our hearts. Here we have a double affirmation. First, salvation in Christ supposes that we be converted to him and away from all that is not Christ, from what St. Paul calls "the law," which according to Luther is all that is exterior to the gospel, to a faith which consists essentially in a total confidence in Christ as Savior and Redeemer and a distrust of oneself. Second, Scripture and Christian doctrine — which have only to do with salvation — do not bring us any speculative knowledge of things. They are oriented purely to helping us make that conversion from the sensible and the worldly to the salvation which is Christ. There is, therefore, a radical difference between philosophy and theology (Christian doctrine); they are of two distinct orders, heterogeneous to each other in such a way that we simply cannot apply our natural knowledge to the science of divine things.

Luther's conviction that it is impossible to apply our natural knowledge of nature and the laws of things to divine realities was reinforced for him by the fact of sinful and fallen nature. Salvation is not brought about by an elevation of nature by means of grace but by a pure aversion of natures and by faith alone, *fide sola*. Thus, in Luther there developed an anti-scholastic, anti-rational reaction, reflected, for instance, in his *Disputatio Contra Scholasticam Theologiam.*

The whole task of theology as it had developed from St. Anselm on was thus completely ruined, since its foundation resided in the possibility of applying the conceptions of reason to supernatural realities. Luther called any theology which tried to see a continuity between the things of nature and the order of Christian realities a pure impossibility. He called his theology a *Theologia Gloriae.* For him the effort to grasp the meaning of Christ by sensible forms is in reality one of darkness, since the true Christian finds his wisdom only in the cross.

In place of a theology speculatively constructed, Luther evolved a theology of piety prepared by a textual study of the Scriptures. We cannot know things in themselves, even Christian things; and in addition our objective is to live in and to love Christ. We must leave the vain, empty study of philosophy for the study of theology. And the nucleus of this is a piety or feeling whereby one does not view objects of knowledge as abstract intelligibles, but rather adheres to them by a consoling and a warm faith. It is a theology of conversion to Christ in a *fiducialis desperatio sui* in the Savior. It is a theology constantly looking back to an interior experience of a conversion from false reality to adherence to the only true reality, Christ. Christ has two natures, what does that matter to me? This type of theology is realized above all in religious acts of faith and prayer; we must not read the Bible like the scholastics "for the sake of a kind of historic knowledge of the Scriptures." Rather, the preparation and diffusion of this theology must be rooted in a study principally directed to the text of Scripture as well as to the texts of the Fathers, above all, those of St. Augustine. For such a program, literary studies are necessary as well as knowledge of ancient languages. It is here that Luther and the Reform sympathized with Erasmus and the humanists. Luther continued to the end of his life a certain study of logic, rhetoric, dialectics, and philosophy. But even here he remained an exaggerated Augustinian. He was of the Augustinian tradition (he was an Augustinian monk) and as such treated these subjects as preparations for the spirit of contemplation. In certain texts, he even stated that philosophy is beneficial but affirmed just as strongly that this philosophy cannot enter into a construction of theology.

Thus Luther gave birth to a sort of double posterity which will be opposed one to the other; they can both be legitimately traced to him alone. From one point Luther has interiorized the Christian principle, giving to theology spiritual criteria for evaluating the experience of salvation; this tendency, reflected for instance in Schleiermacher, gave rise to a "theology of experience" according to which "dogmatics" has as its objective to describe and systematize religious experience. On the other hand, by adhering to the objective data of Christianity — Scripture and the ancient symbols — Luther systematized it according to a dialectic of radical opposition between our world and God, the law and the Gospel. He is recognized as the Father of a "dialectical theology" which is animated by the rejection of all *analogia entis* and of all "supernatural" which is not God Himself.

Thus in the fourteenth and fifteenth centuries there occurred a breakdown of the use of reason within the context of theology. In Roman Catholicism this gave rise to an abstractionism from which the Church of our day still suffers. This was evidenced in the way that many problems of the world-Church relationship were discussed at Vatican II. Many of the Fathers had some very fine abstract concepts of "society," "order and law," "war and revolution," etc. But the rationalistic constitutions of yesterday's moral theology textbooks simply cannot be found in today's world of guerrilla and nuclear warfare, offensive and defensive deterrents, geopolitics and the moral order, international balance of payments and trade agreements for underdeveloped nations, etc. To face these issues realistically, it is necessary to be concretely informed in demography, economics, political science (empirical as well as theoretical), etc. Moreover, the revolution of rising expectations will not, cannot, be amenable to the traditional abstractionalism of the past. Here it is encouraging to note a progress at the highest level in the Church, for the Commission which Pope Paul set up to discuss the question of Christian marriage and birth control was not simply composed of theologians who had been nurtured on the abstract principles of "natural law" (from which are to be deduced all practical principles of action), but also of lay people and various scientists who are familiar with the facts which have a direct or indirect effect on the evolution of this doctrine in the Church today: demography, medicine, economics as well as moral theology.

Vatican II was a step into the modern world, putting aside "essences" to dwell on the empirical experiences of man. Unless it makes this adaptation to modern culture, the Church is doomed to failure and irrelevance in addressing herself to the problems and needs of the men of our day. Our language is so poverty stricken in reference to this task that this alone is one of the most serious obstacles to any kind of a meaningful *aggiornamento*. On the whole we speak a language which men today do not understand. This language cannot express the empirical realities of man today. This is a most serious situation for the Church since she cannot conduct a true dialogue with the world, for the simple reason that the means of communication are not present to her. She speaks of "God," a word which has so little or so distorted a meaning for twentieth-century men; she speaks of "transubstantiation" and the silence is deafening; she speaks of the "essence" of man and of nature, where modern man speaks of his historicity; she speaks of the brotherhood of man, and the modern world speaks of the balance of geopolitics; she speaks of peace while nations of East and West speak of ideological crusades. One could go on and on, and yet it is precisely for this reason that Vatican II is so crucially important for the Church (and really, for the world as well).

This language has been handed down to us from another era, from another cultural expression of human experience and, as such, is *Zeitgebunden*. For human language, like the experience it expresses, and, as it were, incarnates, is limited by these same cultural factors since every human experience is essentially limited by time and space as is every theological system which attempts to synthesize the relationship of this experience to God.

Human thought is essentially evolutionary and historical since what is past experience in mankind's history cannot be experienced today by men of a different age in the same way and in the same circumstances. Human knowledge and experience are growing and widening our field of vision. Thus we are confronted with a new world with its unique experiences and advances of knowledge, and unless the Church can shake off the cultural experience of a former age and adapt God's eternal word ("which remains forever") to this new experience, then God must continue to remain "dead" to the men outside the Church. We remain, then, simply as relics of the past. The new experience of mankind, the "signs of our times" and the social and cultural revolutions have rocked to its very roots the traditional view of the relationship of man to the world in which he lives. No less a revolution is needed in the empirical and terminological modes of expression of the Church. This was the full impact of what Pope John was trying to get across to the Council Fathers of Vatican II when he opened the council by commenting on the essential *aggiornamento* which the Church must undertake today as its most solemn duty and obligation:

> In the daily exercise of Our Pastoral Office, it sometimes happens that we hear certain opinions which disturb us — opinions expressed by people who, though fired with a commendable zeal for religion, are lacking in sufficient prudence and judgment in their evaluation of events. They can see nothing but calamity and disaster in the present state of the world. They say over and over that this modern age of ours, in comparison with past ages, is definitely deteriorating. One would think that history, that great teacher of life, had taught them nothing. They seem to imagine that in the days of the earlier councils everything was as it should be so far as doctrine and morality and the Church's rightful liberty are concerned.
>
> We feel that we must disagree with these prophets of doom, who are always forecasting worse disasters, as though the end of the world were at hand.
>
> Present indications are that the human family is on the threshold of a new era. We must recognize here the hand of God, who, as the years roll by, is ever directing men's efforts, whether they realize it or not, toward the fulfillment of the inscrutable designs of His province, wisely arranging everything, even adverse human fortune, for the Church's good.
>
> . . . .
>
> We have the immense consolation of knowing that the Church, freed at last from worldly fetters that trammeled her in past ages, can through you raise her majestic and solemn voice from this Vatican Basilica, as from a second Apostolic Cenacle.
>
> . . . .
>
> If this doctrine [of the Church] is to make its impact on

> the various spheres of human activity — in private, family and social life — then it is absolutely vital that the Church shall never for an instant lose sight of that sacred patrimony of Truth inherited from the Fathers. But it is equally necessary for her to keep up to date with the changing conditions of this modern world, and of modern living, for these have opened up entirely new avenues for the Catholic Apostolate.
>
> . . . .
>
> Our duty is not just to guard this treasure, as though it was some museum piece and we the curators, but earnestly and fearlessly to dedicate ourselves to the work that needs to be done in this modern age of ours, pursuing the path which the Church has followed for almost twenty centuries.
>
> . . . .
>
> What is needed, and what everyone imbued with a truly Christian, Catholic and Apostolic spirit craves today, is that that doctrine shall be more widely known, more deeply understood, and more penetrating in its effects on men's moral lives. What is needed is that this certain and immutable doctrine to which the faithful owe obedience, *be studied afresh and reformulated in contemporary terms. For this deposit of faith,* or *truths which are contained in our time-honored teaching is one thing; the manner in which these truths are set forth* (*with their meaning preserved intact*) *is something else.* (italics mine)
>
> Thus venerable brethren in the episcopate, "our heart is wide open to you." Here we are assembled in this Vatican Basilica at a turning point in the history of the Church.

The challenge of the Pope is immense and, one might as well say it, revolutionary, for it implies a whole new frame of reference for the position of the Church in the modern world. It is at once a challenge and a task: a task, since the relationship of the Church to the world and its relevancy within it are part of her constitution as willed by Christ; a challenge, since the Church is a human institution (as well as divine). She is subject to human prudence which fears to take on the new and discard the old when it no longer has any meaning for the men to whom the Church addresses her message.

In a sense, this is exactly what the "new theologians" are talking about in the "honest to God" debates now taking place throughout the Anglo-Saxon world. It was, after all, only a short while ago that philosophers in their turn were repeating the famous phrase of Friedrich Nietzsche that "God is dead." The cry is taken up today by theologians who claim that Christian thought must proceed without any reference to God in the traditional sense of the word, since the term is meaningless today. This God of past experience no longer speaks to the modern man since his experiences are far different from, say, those of men in the past.

These new radical theologies are obviously exaggerations, but they do stress the essential point which Pope John was trying to get across to the Council Fathers, namely, that if we cannot make this present transition in experience and formulization, then indeed God will remain a stranger to modern man, God will be dead to them. The main objects of these new "radical theologies" are those which we have already discussed: they assert the unreality of the "death" of God. For modern man to speak of a divine or otherwise supernatural force is meaningless and irrelevant because such "God language" is not related to contemporary experience. It used to be possible to say, for instance, that we cannot know God until He had made Himself known to us, and at that point analogies from the world of personal experience and relations would enter the scene and help us to clarify our notions of God. This situation has entirely deteriorated, since He has not made Himself known to us in the personal experiences and relationships which we have today in the world in which we live. The Church and theology have their work cut out in a way undreamed of since the time when Christianity confronted the Greco-Roman civilization and adapted its words, expressions, and experiences to express its own dogmas and insights into the mystery of the living God.

Thus, in this sense, these new theologies should be regarded as the first attempt to accomplish this mission. They try to give expression within the Church to the secular-technical mind of the twentieth century with which theology must deal if it is to communicate with this new mind.

The new theologians (most of whom are Protestant) have perhaps given some very poor answers, but they have posited the correct questions for the men of religious thought. It cannot be denied, I think, that it is along these basic questions that John XXIII asked the Council Fathers to think. It is to be a positive endeavor above all, since the Church and the world have had enough condemnations by the Church of the new world of modern man.

Language, then, is symbolic of man's present experience; consequently the formulization of religious truths must reflect the way in which man experiences the world, his fellowmen, and God. It will always be partial and imperfect, just as is the human condition. It must be within the culture of our era that religious ideas and symbolisms must become incarnate if religion is to be relevant and meaningful for the men of our day and age. Religion, for man, cannot be disincarnate or unrelated to the culture in which he lives; on the contrary, man worships what he knows, man offers what he is to the deity who reveals himself in an analogical way through the life and experience of man. Psychologically and linguistically, any other conclusion could make no sense.

The ancients recognized this same phenomenon when they said that when God reveals himself, he must do so in the forms and realities which man can understand and in that sense the infinite is limited by the finitude of his finite creatures. Consequently, unless this is recast into such finite but real representations of man's experience today, the eternal verities are in grave danger of making no sense to men today since they do not correspond to this new experience. It is true that God's word has a transcendental quality — precisely because it is God's word — above and beyond the fluctuations of culture and expressions; yet it can become meaningful to men *hic et nunc* only by a sort of continuous incarnation into new forms expressing new experiences so that these divine truths can be captured and increased, as it were, in robes of another culture and experience. Otherwise God's word will fail to be recognized. This function, of course, remains the most solemn function of the Church for each age and culture. Each such period, of course, marks a period of crisis and of transaction in the Church. This was true in the early Church when St. Paul had to, as it were, force a break with the synagogue and its submission to the law and circumcision. It almost created a schism even then. This was true as well during the period of the early Councils when the Church began to explain Christian dogma in the formulas of the Greco-Roman period. It is the same today as the Church attempts to break from the mentality which tended to identify the Christian faith with a particular western cultural expression. Even the great Belloc made this fatal error in his often repeated expression: "The faith is Europe and Europe is the faith." Nothing could be more damaging for the catholicity of the Church since, *de facto*, we face a new world where the modern problems of religious liberty, war and peace, the economic order of the day, poverty, etc., must be confronted within a Christian view. Today is also a period of prudent trial and some mistakes are to be expected. This requires patience and freedom on the side of both the authority in the Church and those subject to this authority. The mentality of the inquisition, of witch-hunting and condemnation must give way to a patient seeking and dialogue within the Church. This is what Pope John meant when he said:

> The Church has always opposed . . . errors, and often condemned them with utmost severity. Today, however, Christ's bride prefers the balm of mercy to the arm of severity. She believes that present needs are best served by explaining more fully the support of her doctrines, rather than by publishing condemnations.

Thus, this expression of the divine mysteries and its transition from ancient formulas to new expression is one of the most momentous tasks of the Church of our day. This was fully recognized by Pope Paul VI in his encyclical, *Mysterium Fidei*. The Pope here recognizes that we have the greatest need for this work not only on the part of theologians but also on the part of the masses of Christians who have, for the most part, mentally rejected this union or else live in a type of permanent schism between their religious beliefs and the new world of our day with its own culture and experience. When this happens, we have a clear case of "departmentalized religion" which is disastrous for the Christian Faith. Pope John once again recognized this when he wrote in *Pacem in terris:*

> It is beyond question that in the creation of those (temporal) institutions many contributed and continue to contribute who were believed to be and who consider themselves Christians; and without a doubt, in part at least, they were and are. How does one explain this? It is our opinion that the explanation is to be found in an inconsistency in their minds between religious belief and their action in the temporal sphere. It is necessary, therefore, that their interior unity be re-established . . . (par. 152).

In a more direct way, this is the burning issue with regard to the missionary endeavor of the Church. The new churches of the Afro-Asian world are complete strangers to the cultural experience and expression of the European-Latin-Constantinian era.

IV

We are confronted with a new era of humanism in which man is defined differently from how he was defined in past ages. The humanism of the Constantinian era was static and logical. It defined man by the abstractions of "nature" and "essence," much as a logician would dissect a principle, deriving from it the component parts. It was abstracted from the determining and influencing features of race, geography, education, etc. Thus there developed a natural law without historical evolution and insensitive to concrete conditions and situations. Man was not a history but an essence. We have a type of "fixation" of the eternal law for all men, in all places, for all times to come where man does not and cannot change the "essence" of his being. The idealistic concept of "person" takes on a platonic essence, a philosophical-juridical-theological determinism unaffected by the political evolution of men from slavery to feudal emancipation in the economic era of the twelfth to thirteenth centuries, by the great modern political incarnation of "person" in the declarations of rights and independence (eighteenth to nineteenth centuries), and by the movement of freedom of the proletariat of the ninteenth and twentieth centuries. All these dynamic evolutionary and political movements were influenced very little by the notion of "person" during this whole Constantinian period, and this explains some of the great difficulties among certain Catholics in accepting the doctrine of religious liberty recently promulgated by Vatican II. The document must be understood from a historical-political point of view as well as from a theological perspective. It is tributary of the vast currents of political influence (limitation of government, declaration and bill of rights, etc.) of over 700 years plus the result of a theological reflection on Scripture and faith. Yet the document makes it clear that the derivative term of "person" is no longer that of the "essential" philosophy of the Middle Ages but is vastly influenced by the historical-political evolution of this term in the secular history of modern man. *The Constitution on the Church in the Modern World*, promulgated at the final session of Vatican II, also reflected this freedom of the person vis-à-vis the elements of this world when it dealt with the economic and industrial structures of our day.

What should be quite clear at this point is that for all practical purposes the modern age has left behind every vestige of a platonic consideration of matter as either an evil or, at least, as something to be shunned as interfering with contemplation of eternal ideas. For modern man, matter is that by which he expresses himself, by which he creates and develops himself. Marx caught this glimpse when he said that man, the *homo faber*, can be defined by work, for in the historical process, man goes out of himself to create a human culture from a brute culture by means of work. Man is not separated from matter, but engaged within it as an incarnate spirit who uses matter as his creative expression. The dualism of Gnosticism and philosophical Platonism, Docetism, Manichaeism, Puritanism, and similar movements considered matter either as an evil or as something to be shunned as an impediment to the full spiritual development of man. This infection of Christian thought is not dead and has led to some deleterious effects on Christian thinking, particularly in its relationship to the modern, industrialized technical world of our day. Christianity has long been infected with a type of crypto-Manichaeism which has considered the material world as well as the tasks within it unworthy of serious consideration by the Christian. This crypto-Gnosticism must be totally discarded if the schism of the Christian vis-à-vis the modern world is to be healed. In Christian circles there has been a constant temptation to make little of these human activities and temporal realities. All dualist doctrines which consider matter the work of an evil principle yield to this temptation.

This, of course, is directly contrary to biblical anthropology where man is seen as Lord of the universe, as God's lieutenant furthering the original act of creation given by means of his reason and industry. Man's activity, in biblical terminology, is a type of continuous creation over brute nature in order to produce a cultural nature of service and rationality. St. Paul, for instance, definitely mentions a certain duality between "flesh" (*sarx*) and "spirit" (*pneuma*). For him, however, the word "spirit" means primarily God Himself as communicated to men. The word is also used in reference to man insofar as he uses all of his faculties according to the designs and wishes of God. It signifies, more particularly, the intelligence of man illuminated by the gift of God, by His divine grace. "Pneumatic," then, means that all of man's faculties (inclusive of his mind, body, desires, tendencies) are used according to God's plan and will. It does not mean the "intellectual" as opposed to the "physical," the immaterial as opposed to the material. On the contrary, a proud man may be very intellectual philosophically but he is by no means spiritual, since his intelligence is not guided by the Holy Spirit but by his egoism and pride. Even the body and its desires are "spiritual," when, for example, the Christian abstains from fornication since his body is the temple of the Holy Spirit (1 Cor 2:10–16). By "flesh" St. Paul and other New Testament writers as well designated those who are led not by the Spirit but by their own egoism, their own light of reason, by their own desires and wishes as opposed to those of God. "Flesh" is all that resists the kingdom of the Spirit. It is not the equivalent of flesh in the sense of physical reality. As a matter of fact, in the Epistle to the Galatians, St. Paul makes a summary list of the works of the flesh (5:19–21). Among these are found some things that are in no way "flesh" in the physical sense, e.g., envy, hate, disputes, dissensions, etc.

Thus, this distinction of the Bible is in no way to be confused with the Greek-Gnostic dualist conceptions of "body-soul" and the dichotomy between the realities signified by these concepts — a confusion that was introduced early in Christianity (e.g., Gnosticism, Manichaeism, Docetism, Iranian, Mandaeian influences, etc.) and has not as yet been carefully weeded out of Christian attitudes. As a matter of fact, Semitic thought (on which St. Paul and St. John are dependent) knew of no such dichotomy. Paul's and John's analysis is not that of the Greek philosophers of matter (body) and of the principle (soul), nor could it be. *A fortiori,* neither St. Paul nor any of the writers of the New Testament ever conceived of any type of gnostic dualism where the soul is imprisoned in a quasi-evil principle, the body or matter. For the writers of the New Testament, the body was simply an integral part of man, who was created as one whole by God, destined entirely either for eternal life or eternal death. This point is central, for it radically distinguishes the thought of the Bible from all types of Greek philosophy as well as from extraneous, religious, gnostic influences. The cosmos is good, created as it was by God and destined for the service of man, God's lieutenant in this creation. This contrasts, perhaps, with a segment of Catholic thought which has been influenced too much by Greek philosophy and not nourished enough from the sources of revelation. Unconsciously, at least, Greek influence has led to a depreciation of human and temporal values in Christian life. And this depreciation has been the source of a certain impoverishment of the sense of God's presence in temporal affairs and matters.

During the pontificate of John XXIII, this temptation was fully and courageously confronted, especially in his encyclical

Mater et Magistra. John emphatically declared that the material universe and the material labor of mankind are willed by God. Furthermore, this world which we see and touch has been recreated by the Incarnation of the Son of God. By reason of his nature, man stands on the horizon between matter and spirit. In the beautiful words of St. Hilary, "He is the bond of friendship uniting and glorifying all creation." Consequently, the Christian vocation of the layman to and in the world is to establish the kingdom of Christ within the modern world. Christians must engage themselves in the task of this world with each other above all, but also with all men of good will. Christian perfection is inconceivable without temporal engagement in the tasks, problems, and agonies of modern man. Always conscious of the fact that they are members of the family of God, Christians must all the more be conscious and perceptive of justice in the world of man, always striving to make this world a better place to live, a habitat of justice, and a world worthy of the sacred being who is man. This is what the Pope calls "socialization" and as such it is the sacred divine-human vocation of the layman.

> Hence, when Christians put themselves to work — even if it be in a task of temporal nature — in conscious union with the Divine redeemer, every effort becomes a continuation of the effort of Jesus Christ and is penetrated with redemptive power: "He who abides in Me and I in him, he bears much fruit." It thus becomes a more exalted and more noble labor, one which contributes to a man's personal and spiritual perfection, helps to reach out and impart to others on all sides the fruits of Christian redemption. It further follows that the Christian message leavens, as it were, with the ferment of the Gospel, the civilization in which one lives and works.

Thus in Pope John we have turned a big corner in the healing of the spiritual schism which has separated the Christian from the modern world.

This leads us directly into another phase of the Constantinian era which has been heavily modified by the modern era, namely, the concept of man and his purpose in history. The former era is known as the epoch of Christian humanism at its fullest where, as we have said, man is defined by his "nature," an abstraction made from particular individuals, race, geography, and education: man is absolutely the same everywhere. All this is a far cry from biblical anthropology, which stresses the direct, personal call (vocation) to each sacred human person by the personal Lord of history. When the notion of an abstract human nature is linked to a philosophy of man as body and soul, the way is set for a profound dichotomy in the mind of the Christian which has not been healed to this day. This has been noted in present Christian circles in the traditional (at least from St. Augustine's time) notions of sexuality and the corresponding treatment of marriage in theology. Above all, it is reflected in the continuous schism of the Christian as he has faced the birth of a new culture, a new civilization built squarely on the rationalization of matter by industry and technology. The modern world seems to be saying to the Church before it will accept its remedies and ministry: "Physician, heal yourself." It is within this industrial-technical world that the Christian must, for better or for worse, find the fulfillment of his vocation.

In our construction of a new Christian approach for a new era, it will be far more profitable and truthful to avoid, in reference to the secular city, such terms as "Christian" philosophy or "Christian" economy or "Christian" politics for the rather simple reason (aside from the fact that each of these realities has its own dynamism and goal, quite independent of any Christian influence *qua* Christian influence) that each of these realities includes within itself an extreme relativism by groups, time, social milieu, etc.; and it would be erroneous to see in all or in any one of them a type of ahistorical, atemporal existence for men of all time to come and for each future epoch. The men of the Constantinian era never even dreamed of a situation when pluralism would be the rule and Christians in the minority, and they consequently had no corresponding theology for such an eventuality; in truth, the Constantinian era had no consciousness of man's historicity. In a sense, the tension between the earthly and the eternal city became almost nonexistent within this

"Christendom." This explains perhaps much of Christian nostalgia for an idealized past.

The Church of our day has learned a real, even if painful, lesson in this respect over the past 100 years; as she has seen her privileged position in the state and culture erode, she has lately begun to see moral possibilities open to her which were never dreamed of by the reactionary nineteenth century. Freed from the fetters of the constraining Constantinian Church-State relations, she now has the evangelical freedom to judge each culture, each state; she has become no longer a public political power but rather, in keeping with her evangelical origin, a moral power to influence men and events for good. Thus Pope John reminded the fathers of Vatican II that:

> We have the immense consolation of knowing that the Church, freed at last from the worldly fetters that trammelled her in past ages, can through you raise her majestic and solemn voice . . .

Freed from any particular culture and its expressions, she has the freedom of adapting to each and being confused by none. She experiences a freedom today in her universal, moral, and catholic dimensions that simply has not been hers for over 1600 years of this whole past Constantinian era.

This will also give the Church the necessary freedom to accept other temporal expressions of man's cultural creation. *De facto*, this has been the policy of the Church during the past seventy years, during which she has attempted to humanize the temporal economic order of modern times. Even here we see an evolution of thought with regard to, say socialism, where we proceed from simple and total condemnation (Pius IX, Leo XIII) to a distinction in types (Pius XI, Pius XII) to an approval when the circumstances have evolved in this respect (John XXIII, Paul VI). Changes in philosophical systems, sociology, family structures, and political institutions have all produced a corresponding change and development in the Church's teachings in each of these fields. The present debate on birth control and anovulants is a case in point of a progressive realization that family structures have reached a new development in the automated, urbanized society in which we live.

This corresponds and must correspond to a rethinking by the Church of traditional teachings which were conceptualized for another age of man, dominated by rural and agricultural interests. This influence of culture and milieu is not simply extrinsic; it is of intrinsic importance in grasping how man develops historically and how he better understands himself and his environment and his relationship to it. An understanding of contemporary culture requires not simply an external adaptation of Church teaching, but an intrinsic investigation into its correspondence to a new situation, a new knowledge of man by man. If the Church wishes truly to become incarnational, influencing men for good *from within*, then she must attempt to incarnate the evangelical message within these changed, temporal structures. It is exactly here that we shall have either a true *aggiornamento* or continue to mark time by making superficial changes without modifying the basic structures of the Church. If the latter course is pursued we will continue to be outside the problems of the new cultural world in which men live here and now.

It should be clear from Sacred Scripture that Christian faith is not restricted to any culture, any particular politics, sociology, philosophy, or any other temporal structures in which the evangelical message must become incarnate if it is to be relevant and meaningful to men of any particular time and place. It is precisely in these existing structures that she must become incarnate. If not, the Church will remain apart from the world, and this has been the case for the past two hundred years, above all, in the industrial-technical milieu of the modern world.

In a sense, there will always be a certain tension in the relationship of the Church with the world. On the one hand, we have the absolute imperative of the Church to be faithful to the deposit given to her once and for all by her divine Founder; on the other, there is the divine imperative to save the world as it is in each age. This requires a continual adaptation and rethinking of the gospel, and this always runs a risk, not from the point of view of faith (since the Church is guaranteed essential fidelity to the evangelical message by the abiding Spirit within her through her adequate *Magisterium*); but from the point of view of the all too human subjects of the Church, they can come to identify her and the faith with one or another particularizing temporal structural whole in which Christianity has at any one time become incarnate. This has happened many times in the life of the Church.

This failure was continued after Trent which was, after all, a period of defense and retrenchment. Some reforms were realized — but a sweeping reform of ecclesial structure was not attempted, with the result that the Church was not prepared in any way to meet the even more revolutionary period of the seventeenth to twentieth centuries. She retreated in the face of this revolutionary period into a ghetto where even her moral system suffered a complete breakdown in adjusting to the social realities of the times, brought about by the socialization (understood in the Johannine sense) of society. We have here the encouragement of the Christian away from the world (the place of evil and temptation) to the realm of spiritual activity where he could "save his soul." The morality of social structures was simply abandoned to an easier method of working out one's salvation by individual sacramental frequentation, pious practices, and keeping away "from the world."

The result was ruinous both for the world as well as for the Christian since the world was left to its own ideologies with which to organize itself and the Christian, instead of influencing it from within, stood outside sometimes condemning it (materialism), sometimes relegating it to the unimportant. A mental and spiritual schism resulted. Thus the social morality which the Church should have been developing vis-à-vis this growing and revolutionary world was abandoned to those whose vision did not include real religious principles and connotations (Physiocrats, Socialists, Marxists, Libertarian Capitalists, etc.). This spirit is not yet dead since it still seems that the ultimate criterion of a "good" Catholic is attendance at religious functions and frequent reception of the sacraments — especially in the American Church. Yet, this is but half of religion whose connotation must make its effect on the sociotemporal structures of man, where, for better or for worse, man draws his values and morals. It is only the exceptional man or Christian who can fully resist the influence of his milieu.

Today, many of the political, sociological, philosophical, and cultural attitudes of another age have hindered the Church from incarnating the evangelical message into a new culture, new attitudes, new *Weltanschauungen*. The modern world has been left to swim for itself, left to its own inner dynamics and variant ideologies. This was and continues to be a grave defeat for the Church, since no culture and no civilization is, a *priori*, incapable of being the human framework and receptacle of divine grace. While it is true that many elements of this past epoch of the Church are still capable of expressing the divine message, many others are not, surrounded as they are by certain temporally limited attitudes. These have long since lost their effectiveness for the men of our day. For that reason they are moribund and will be detrimental if continued any longer. We see this very clearly in the traditional concept of Church-State relations and above all in the sacralization of the political-sociological order. Other aspects are disappearing which in their time served the Church well, but are being taken over by the fully developed and conscious secular society of the modern age (education, organized charity, diaconal duties and services, etc.). This aspect will be studied in a further chapter.

Each epoch, if the Church is to be faithful to the imperatives of her Savior, needs the Church for its Christianizing and humanizing influences. To deny this, it seems to me, is to deny the incarnational mission of the Church to the world. But no particular epoch can be identified with the Church as such, no matter how rich it might seem to be. This is so because the Church is the continuous Incarnation of Christ through all the ages of men for all time to come and men do change as a historical fact. It is of service to man (and not vice versa), to every epoch with its own cultural, social, and economic expression. The dogmatic *Constitution on the Church* of Vatican II has made this abundantly clear in many of its passages:

> ... while (the Church) transcends all limits of time and confines of race, the Church is destined to extend to all regions of the earth and so enters into the history of mankind. Moving forward through trial and tribulation, the Church is strengthened by the power of God's grace, which was promised to her by the Lord, so that in the weakness of the flesh she may not waver from perfect fidelity, but remain a bride worthy of her Lord, and moved by the Holy Spirit may never cease to renew herself, until through the Cross she arrives at the light which knows no setting (par. 9).
>
> Since the Kingdom of Christ is not of this world, the Church or people of God in establishing that Kingdom takes nothing away from the temporal welfare of any people. On the contrary, it fosters and takes to itself, insofar as they are good, the ability, riches and customs in which the genius of each people expresses itself; taking them to itself it purifies, strengthens, elevates and ennobles them. The Church in this is mindful that she must bring together the nations for that King to whom they were given as an inheritance, and to whose city they bring gifts and offerings. This characteristic of universality which adorns the people of God is a gift from the Lord Himself. By reason of it, the Catholic Church strives constantly and with due effect to bring all humanity and all its possessions back to its source in Christ . . . (par. 13).
>
> Through (the Church's) work, whatever good is in the minds and hearts of men, whatever good lies latent in the religious practices and cultures of diverse peoples, is not only saved from destruction but is also cleansed, raised up and perfected unto the glory of God, the confusion of the devil and the happiness of man (par. 17).
>
> In this way (the laity) may make Christ known to others, especially by the testimony of a life resplendent in faith, hope, and charity. Therefore, since they are tightly bound up in all types of temporal affairs, it is their special task to order and throw light upon these affairs in such a way that they may come into being and then continually increase according to Christ . . . (par. 31).
>
> The faithful, therefore, must learn the deepest meaning and value of all creation, as well as its role in the harmonious praise of God. They must assist each other to live holier lives even in their daily occupations. In this way the world may be permeated by the spirit of Christ and it may more effec-

> tively fulfill its purpose in justice, charity, and peace. The laity have the principal role in the overall fulfillment of this duty. Therefore, by their competence in secular training and by their activity, elevated from within by the grace of Christ, let them vigorously contribute their effort, so that created goods may be perfected by human labor, technical skill and civic culture for the benefit of all men according to the design of the creator and the light of His Word. May the goods of this world be more equitably distributed among all men, and may they in their own way be conducive to universal progress in human and Christian freedom. In this manner, through the members of the Church, will Christ progressively illuminate the whole of human society with His saving light. Moreover, let the laity also by their combined efforts remedy the customs and conditions of the world, if they are an inducement to sin, so that they all may be conformed to the norms of justice and may favor the practice of virtue rather than hinder it. By so doing they will imbue culture and human activity with genuine moral values; and they will better prepare the field of the world for the seed of the Word of God (par. 36).

These passages could be multiplied. They are reflected in the *Pastoral Constitution on the Church in the Modern World.* The principle was clearly set forth for the Church at Vatican II. We here have now definitely gone beyond the moribund Constantinian era. We mark here, at least in principle, the end of one era and the beginning of another for the Church. For, after all, the Constantinian era was itself simply *one* expression or extension of a particular social, cultural, and economic pattern. We have passed to new expressions, to a new era, the revolutionary and modern era of the industrial-technical rationalization of the world. Thus, as the Council itself attests to, a temporal and incarnational engagement of the Church — that is, a temporal organization including what Christians do here below in order to realize among men a transportation and conditioning of individual and social morality — is an absolute necessity for the Church today for its own relevance to and for the modern world. It is a contingent as well as a permanently enduring challenge for the Church of every age and for all times to come. It must be *the* task of the Church for each epoch so that the Incarnation of Christ in the Church can continue in the world "until He comes."

V

Thus this new incarnation of the Church into the modern world is both a challenge (and hence, a risk) as well as a magnificent opportunity for the birth of new hope in the new era. The appearance of a Pope at the U. N. General Assembly was at once a symbol for the Church as well as a hope for the world. It was a symbol insofar as the Church in the person of her most prominent member here on earth appeared before men as humble, aligned with no temporal power whatsoever, whose only desire was to be of service to them in the cause of peace and justice; it expressed hope for the world insofar as here in the world's midst was one who had nothing to gain in a material or political way, one man (in whose person is represented the Church itself) who was above all others disinterested in all earthly power and who encompassed all, East and West alike, as one common father encompasses his wrangling children. His speech might well serve as the Magna Carta for the new function of the Church in a new world. Thus the words of Paul VI:

> This encounter [at the U.N.], as you understand, marks a simple and at the same time a great moment. It is simple because you have before you a humble man, your brother, and among you all, representatives of sovereign states, the least vested, if you wish to think of him. Thus, with a miniscule, as it were symbolic, temporal sovereignty, only as much as is necessary to be free to exercise his spiritual mission, and to assure all those who deal with him that he is independent of every other sovereignty of this world. But he who addresses you has no temporal power, nor any ambition to compete with you. In fact, we have nothing to ask for, no question to raise; we have only a desire to express and a permission to request; namely that of serving you insofar as we can, with disinterest, with humility, and with love.
>
> . . . .
>
> We said also, however, and all here today feel it, that this moment is also a great one. Great for us, great for you. For

> us, you know who we are. Whatever may be the opinion you have of the Pontiff of Rome, you know our mission. We are the bearer of a message for all mankind. And this we are, not only in our own personal name and in the name of the great Catholic family; but also in that of those Christian brethren who share the same sentiment, which we express here, particularly of those who so kindly charged us explicitly to be their spokesmen here. Like a messenger who, after a long journey, finally succeeds in delivering the letter which has been entrusted to him, so we appreciate the good fortune of this moment, however brief, which fulfills a desire nourished in the heart for nearly twenty centuries. For, as you will remember, we are very ancient; we here represent a long history; we here celebrate the epilogue of a wearying pilgrimage in search of a conversation with the entire world, ever since the command was given to us: go and bring the good news to all peoples. Now, you here represent all peoples. Allow us to tell you that we have a message, a happy message, to deliver to each one of you and to all.
>
> . . . .
>
> The hour has struck for our "conversion," for personal transformation, for interior renewal. We must get used to thinking of man in a new way; and in a new way also of men's life in common; with a new manner too of conceiving the paths of history and the destiny of the world. . . . the hour has struck for a halt, a moment of recollection, of reflection, almost of prayer. A moment to think anew of our common origin, our history, our common destiny. Today as never before, in our era so marked by human progress, there is need for an appeal to the moral conscience of man. For the danger comes, not from progress, nor from science — indeed, if properly used, these could rather resolve many of the grave problems which assail mankind. No, the real danger comes from man himself, yielding ever more powerful instruments which could be equally employed for destruction or for the loftiest conquests.

This talk of Paul VI must certainly rank with Pope John XXIII's talk to Vatican II as one of the classical pieces as the Church now attempts to bring about a new *aggiornamento* in its incarnation into the modern world. A new position, a new moral force *within* the world, not a preaching to or condemnation of the world. Here the Church reaches the fullness of her evangelical mission among men in its most pure form: to be of service out of love to the world, guiding it in its own way to an earthly realm of justice, peace, and love — insofar as that is given to men here below. Here, in the person of the Pope, the Church stands with and among men, sharing their problems and agonies, comforting them in their discouragement, encouraging them when they are weak, continuously reminding them of their common brotherhood — in short, a true incarnational Christianity for our day in service and love. Paul VI has given the Church the perfect road on which the Church must travel among men if she is to be relevant and helpful to them. The fruits, then, of the new Johannine era are significantly begun and given to us by his successor who, in one concrete action, has brilliantly illuminated the way to John's *aggiornamento*. It is hard to exaggerate the significance of Paul's action at the U. N.; along with Vatican II, it opened up a new era for the Church in a new world of new men.

VI

The source of this continuous renewal in the Church is, of course, her constant reference and return to the sacred word of God. It is here that she finds both her strength and her continuous youth by which she approaches and incarnates herself into every age and every culture. Since this word is divine, it has a renovating message for every man for all times, but above all, for the Church of God in whom men must find their salvation here on earth. It is here that she is nourished and strengthened for her perpetually new task in the world wherein she is charged by the divine savior to announce the good news to every creature and thus to live concretely this word in the thousand different ramifications of a temporal engagement, in a new era and in a new culture. As we have seen, Pope John explicitly enjoined this on the Council so that by returning to the pristine freshness of her origins in the Sacred Scripture, she might once again appear as the poor and service-filled handmaid of fallen humanity as it strives in a valley of tears to bring about a temporal (even if imperfect) redemption of itself as willed by Christ for the world.

This renovation of the Church by a return of her origins is not something new in the Church for it has been the constant theme of the various charismatic individuals — prophets and saints — who, as the *Constitution on the Church* reminds us, have never been lacking to the Church during her long history even if heavy administrative bureaucracy of the ecclesiastical structure has given them some very hard times. Their persistence and their approval by the Church has shown them to be the true voices of the Spirit speaking in the Church's midst.

St. Benedict and St. Francis of Assisi come immediately to mind as the most outstanding examples of this evangelical return in the midst of the ecclesial community. In an incipient mercantile age, St. Francis appeared with the simple message of evangelical joy and poverty so that renewal in the Church appeared and became a concrete reality through the new phenomena raised up by the Holy Spirit to incarnate this ever new evangelical message in a simple man from Assisi. Even his followers were called an order of "mendicants" as a sign of the principle of evangelical poverty in the midst of this new civilization of the thirteenth century. Thus a new relationship, a new phenomenon appeared in a new age — new with regard to that particular age but ancient in its return to the moral strength of Christianity, that of the simplicity of evangelical poverty. So too was it with the great charismatics through the new ages of later centuries: St. Teresa of Avila, St. Dominic, St. Ignatius of Loyola, St. Francis de Sales, St. Charles Borromeo, and the beggar of the fully industrial age of the nineteenth century, St. Benedict Lebre.

In each case, the ecclesiastical "establishment" was shaken to its roots by a very simple but earth-shaking reminder of evangelical poverty, humility, service, and, above all, of the fraternal love of her origins in the Gospels, beyond the selfishness and self-satisfied ecclesiastical *status quo* of each epoch into which the charismatics come to disturb, and by disturbing, to make the Church rethink and return to the simple injunction of Christ to love and be of service to the fraternity: "By this shall all men know . . ."

> These charisms, whether they are to be more outstanding or the more simple and widely diffused, are to be received with thanksgiving and consolation for they are perfectly suited to and useful for the needs of the Church (*Constitution on the Church*, par. 12).

Each of these charismatics was and continues to be a reminder to the Church: (1) that she has no abiding city here below; (2) that a rich, "powerful" and "established" Church (understood here in the sense of ecclesiastical concordism of the *status quo* in the cultural, political, and economic order) is not and cannot be an apt means for announcing the simple gospel of justice, poverty, and evangelical, fraternal love to the poor of this world (understood here in the sense of the biblical *anawim*). On the contrary, these worldly implementations and growths become a terrible judgment upon her and a source of needless scandal both for her own faithful as well as for the men outside of her fold among whom she is supposed to be, in the words of Vatican II, "that standard raised up among the nations." This explains, to a great degree at least, the tragedy of the Reformation, ironically called "reformation" for the simple reasons that the Church was not able to reform herself to the Gospel because of the dry rationalism into which she had become encased by identifying herself with the temporal structures of the Middle Ages. It will be remembered that the Fifth Council of the Lateran (1517) had drawn up some magnificent reformatory decrees only to have them remain so many pieces of paper. It was the duty and obligation of the Council of Trent (1563) to react in a defensive gesture which, even if necessary, was not and could not be enough for the Church for the simple reason that it was a negative reaction and not a positive confrontation with a new age and a new world. The reform of the Church remained incomplete and actually receded in the face of an ever expanding and radically changing world of the later seventeenth through twentieth centuries.

In a type of reverse irony, as the Church retreated in an action of self-defense, the world with its own culture, economy, and sociology literally exploded without the Church and sometimes in opposition to her. Vatican II set for itself the momentous task of closing that gap by open dialogue, confrontation, and understanding of that new world and its culture. It marked, in the words of John XXIII, a definite turning point in her history where she is finally in the painful process of shedding the Constantinian-Tridentine attitude of establishment-retrenchment to that of openness, reciprocity, understanding, and service of this transformed society with the new values which have arisen in the consciences of men. The Church has been able to make this break with moribund forms, expressions, and attitudes precisely because of her return to her evangelical origins which originally gave her, for all times to come, the freedom of the Son of God, a complete liberty vis-à-vis all temporal economic, social, political, and cultural forms of any or of all ages to come. The freshness and newness of the evangelical message with which Christ has purchased us is now once again free to be the yeast in the dough, the light on the mountain, the salt of the earth of the new era which is now the temporal receptacle of Christ's grace through the Church. This is the reason why it is so fundamental for the Church to return once again to her scriptural sources if she is to have a renewal for the world of our day. One has only to read some of the official texts of the Council to see this clearly. *The Constitution on the Liturgy* is profoundly biblical at its very base and at every turn. Its introductory paragraphs are illuminating in this respect.

> This sacred Council has several aims in view: it desires to impart an ever-increasing vigor to the Christian life of the faithful; to adapt more suitably to the needs of our own times those institutions which are subject to change; to foster whatever can promote union among all who believe in Christ; to strengthen whatever can help to call the whole of mankind into the household of the Church. The Council therefore sees particularly cogent reasons for undertaking the reform and promotion of the liturgy (par. 1).
>
> For the liturgy, "through which the work of our redemption is accomplished," most of all in the divine sacrifice of the Eucharist, is the outstanding means whereby the faithful may express in their lives, and manifest to others, the mystery of Christ and the real nature of the true Church. It is of the

essence of the Church that she be both human and divine, invisible and yet visibly equipped, eager to act; intent on contemplation, present in this world and yet not at home in it; and she is all these things in such a way that in her the human is directed and subordinated to the divine, the visible likewise to the invisible, action to contemplation, and this present world to that city yet to come, which we seek. While the liturgy daily builds up those who are within into a holy temple of the Lord, into a dwelling place for God in the Spirit, to the mature measure of the fulness of Christ, at the same time it marvelously strengthens their power to preach Christ, and thus shows forth the Church to those who are outside as a sign lifted up among the nations under which the scattered children of God may be gathered together, until there is one sheepfold and one Shepherd (par. 2).

This same teaching permeates the *Constitution on the Church* as well. It is noteworthy how the whole document is biblical in tone and content. The essence of the Church here is the Trinity to which Christians have been united as one family of God, a Church of humility, service, and love — and a dynamic movement away from the juridical notion of the Church which has been prevalent for the past 1000 years. The introductory chapters of this document bring this out very well.

The eternal Father, by a free and hidden plan of his own wisdom and goodness, created the whole world. His plan was to raise men to a participation of the divine life. Fallen in Adam, God the Father did not leave men to themselves, but ceaselessly offered helps to salvation, in view of Christ, the Redeemer "who is the image of the invisible God, the firstborn of every creature." All the elect, before time began, the Father "foreknew and predestined to become conformed to the image of His Son, that he should be the firstborn among many brethren." He planned to assemble in the holy Church all those who would believe in Christ. Already from the beginning of the world the foreshadowing of the Church took place. It was prepared in a remarkable way throughout the history of the people of Israel and by means of the Old Covenant. In the present era of time the Church was constituted and, by the outpouring of the Spirit, was made manifest. At the end of time it will gloriously achieve completion, when, as is read in the Fathers, all the just, from Adam and "from Abel, the just one, to the last of the elect, will be gathered together with the Father in the universal Church" (par. 2).

The Son, therefore, came sent by the Father. It was in Him, before the foundation of the world, that the Father chose us and predestined us to become adopted sons, for in Him it pleased the Father to re-establish all things. To carry out the will of the Father, Christ inaugurated the kingdom of Heaven on earth and revealed to us the mystery of that kingdom. By His obedience He brought about redemption. The Church, or in other words, the kingdom of Christ now present in mystery, grows visibly through the power of God in the world. This inauguration and this growth are both symbolized by the blood and water which flowed from the open side of a crucified Jesus, and are foretold in the words of the Lord referring to His death on the Cross: "And I, if I be lifted up from the earth, will draw all things to Myself." As often as the Sacrifice of the cross in which Christ our Passover was sacrificed is celebrated on the altar, the work of our redemption is carried on, and, in the sacrament of the eucharistic bread, the unity of all believers who form one body in Christ is both expressed and brought about. All men are called to this union with Christ, who is the light of the world, from whom we go forth, through whom we live, and toward whom our whole life strains (par. 3).

When the work which the Father gave the Son to do on earth was accomplished, the Holy Spirit was sent on the day of Pentecost in order that He might continually sanctify the Church, and thus, all those who believe would have access through Christ in one Spirit to the Father. He is the Spirit of life, a fountain of water springing up to life eternal. To men, dead in sin, the Father gives life through Him, until, in Christ, He brings to life their mortal bodies. The Spirit dwells in the Church and in the hearts of the faithful, as in a temple. In them He prays on their behalf and bears witness to the fact that they are adopted sons. The Church, which the Spirit guides in the way of all truth and which He unified in communion and in works of ministry, He both equips and directs with hierarchical and charismatic gifts and adorns with His fruits. By the power of the Gospel He makes the Church keep the freshness of youth. Uninterruptedly, He renews it and leads it to perfect union with its spouse. The Spirit and the Bride both say to Jesus, the Lord, "Come!"

Thus, the Church has been seen as a people made one with the unity of the Father, the Son and the Holy Spirit (par. 4).

These two documents, of course, are only the beginning of the reform within the Church, but it is precisely here that reform must begin and then only can the Church approach the world in the spirit of love and service as did, in fact, Paul VI in his first encyclical *Ecclesiam Suam* as well as in his talk to the U. N. This reformatory movement is continued in the famous *Pastoral Constitution on the Church in the Modern World*, promulgated at the final session of the Council in the fall of 1965.

It is then only in this spirit of renewal by returning to its sources in Sacred Scripture that the Church will find the strength and courage as well as the freedom from the temporal, cultural forms of the Constantinian era and with vigor once again to make a similar effort for a new era in a new world. Thus she fulfills her divine imperative to become the extended Incarnation of God's Word in the midst of this revolutionary world and thereby become the Christian witness of the Incarnate World *within* this new culture, not *alongside* of it; it becomes, moreover, the fermenting grace of Christ preparing and bringing about the divine fraternity of men of our age within our age.

For indeed, within the temporal and historical existence of men, it is only the Word of God which remains forever precisely because it comes from Him who is Lord of History. It alone is supremely free of historicism and the accidental (but temporally necessary for each age) cultural patterns of men and nations and, hence, imposes on the Church, who is its faithful servant, a condition of permanent and everlasting *metanoia* against the mortal blows of an institutionalized, cultural conformity to any particular age. This is the continuous Pentecost which belongs to the Church alone and about which Pope John spoke in his opening address to the Council. This is the holy "dissatisfaction" about which spiritual writers so often speak as well as that of the charismatics throughout the history of the Church. The faith both of the Church as well as that of each person within the Church is independent and free of any particularizing culture or age (*Zeitgeist*) precisely because the faith is a transcendental reality reaching beyond the temporal institutions of men to Him who was, who is, and who will be. Yet, at the same time, the faith has another face, as it were, turned in pity and love toward the temporal institutions where men move and have their being so as to influence them from within with a specific, Christian and humanizing leaven. Thus, faith can be disengaged from moribund aspects of any particular culture without doing violence in any way whatsoever to that faith. In this way it can once again become incarnate within the new cultural, economic, and sociological forms of a new age, in a new world.

It is precisely here that this wisdom of John XXIII shines through (even if there were some inklings from Leo XIII to Pius XII) like a light in the darkness. Without fear (for the Word of God need fear nothing from man or his creations), with great courage (for a whole mentality within the Church has to change and a new one created starting with Vatican II), the Pope opened this dialogue with the industrial-technical, secular, and even atheistic world of the twentieth century. By this stroke of courage which can only be explained by the impulse of the Spirit, the Church is now in an overall position for the first time in over 400 years to begin to influence structurally and win over to Christ this new reality in which she has been living — but as a leaven, not as a belligerent and opposing force. In this sense, the *Constitution on the Church* points out, the whole Church of her very nature is missionary to every age, to all men, and for all times. The mission of the Church must not become a sort of appendix to the life of the Church (par. 17).

One small example should make this quite clear and at the same time should show how difficult it really is for the Christian and the Church to make such a disengagement. The question of the "just war" has been traditional in Catholic theological circles since the very beginnings of the Constantinian era, particularly from the time of St. Augustine who formulated it. The conditions of this type of war were: (1) just authority; (2) just cause; (3) just means; and (4) a just intention. We cannot go into a detailed analysis of this theory as theory. It is enough to say that it was an effort to establish as it were a parallel between war and the legitimate "police" functions of a given government within the sphere of its sovereignty. Medieval Europe did not have a unified government; it did, however, have some sentiment of a cohesive cultural and moral universe; the standards for measurement of the "just war" were, for "Christendom," the moral equivalent of a unified, political order. Thus, these criteria, as traditionally phrased during the Constantinian era, simply pushed the debatable question of war one step further back by saying that the means of waging war should not be intrinsically immoral or should be in accord with the moral nature of man. This "just war" theory presupposed both a morally unified world ("Christendom") and an objective Christian point of judgment (revelation). The judgment of "justice" of the war was understood as an objective, moral evaluation of the war itself, therefore binding on both sides; not as a judgment only on the subjective honesty or the sincerity of the belligerents.

There is no conclusive evidence *whatsoever* that the doctrine of the "just war" was ever actually used as a tool for providing moral guidance to men making actual political choices. There is not on record any case where a "Christian" population of any nation refused to support the national government in the prosecution of a war because that war was unjust. The Crusades, the Inquisition, Colonialism, and Hitler, with the wars these political systems involved, were accepted *unflinchingly* by Christian populations and, in fact, supported enthusiastically by Church leaders in every nation, in spite of the fact that none of them could possibly have met the above-mentioned criteria of a "just war." Wars within Christian Europe went on unabated. The Church — which claimed authority and unity of Christendom — never put its claimed authority to the test by labeling as illegitimate any European war. Thus, in direct contradiction to the criterion that a war can be "just" at most on one side, Catholic Christians fought on both sides of most wars. Theologians, on the other hand, had to uphold the theory at least in theory even if not one Christian ever gave any serious attention to it. The doctrine had to hold at least on paper since theologians had to reject the unqualified *raison d'état* which would consider Christians as obligated to serve the state — whatever it asks for.

Although in practice this was essentially what happened, theologians were aware that such an unbridled ratification of the demands of the state could not be justified doctrinally, and therefore they gave lip service to the need for discrimination. Since historically there is no record of the "just war" theory having been applied negatively, we must conclude that actually it is (and remains today) the *raison d'état* which has dominated in the actual practice of Christians, though not in the meditations of theologians. This historical observation tends to give weight, more than we like to admit, to the argument of some Christian pacifists to the effect that all Christians' participation in war is the result not of differing ethical position (since none whatsoever is recorded), but of a basic option of unconditional loyalty to the nation, or in other words, a result of real idolatry in the biblical sense of the word. From a theological point of view, this is not all that clear, but men do not live out their lives and actions in theological reasonings; what is very certain is that *historically* and *in fact*, the Church has been so identified (in each country) with nationalism that it has failed to lead men in most of their questions since the time of Constantine.

Here is one of the most blatant examples of corrupt witness by the people of the Church, a real failure in the evangelical witness to peace and concord, each local church identifying itself not with the Gospel but with the passions of nationalism. It is, above all, Constantinian in its vision of society as Christianized not by evangelical principles from within, but by the sword. The originality of the message of Jesus in the New Testament (and reinforced by the decree of Vatican II on Religious Liberty), as over against Jewish messianic expectations was His utter rejection of external coercion as a means of moral renewal. After Constantine, particularly after St. Augustine, there was a reversion to the Maccabean concept of the relation of God's people to their world's kingdoms. It was, after all, the normal mode of operating in the Constantinian synthesis or synergism as we have called it at the beginning of this chapter. It is both Constantinian and unbiblical in the fusion of Church and State as ethical agents in the temporal order.

We come to the rather ugly conclusion that if the "just war" theory were in fact true, theologically speaking, then we would have to condemn nearly all the wars in which Christians have willingly participated in the past. This failure to contribute effectively to the process of moral decision constitutes an implicit refutation of the doctrine itself. Yet, even if the doctrine remains true in the abstract, its practical failure to influence the moral conduct of Christians in war shows very clearly the nationalistic chains in which the Church has been held captive since Constantine.

There are other terrible drawbacks to this over-identification resulting in a loss of freedom for the Church in her missionary effort to and for the world. It was the Church of the Constantinian period which created the notion of missionary activity as a special appendage of the Church's activity, as a restrained and specialized function of the Church for the single reason that she identified the Roman-Feudal cultural world with the faith itself and, consequently, became itself a part of this cultural established order (one will remember that before the French Revolution the Church was considered one of the essential parts of the established order along with the king and the nobility). This "establishment" made it psychologically impossible for her to confront and "baptize" the alien cultural patterns of the East. This Romanization in its own turn explains, at least to a great degree, the hardening of schism of the Eastern and Western Church which was already strained long before the final break in 1054. This also explains to a very large degree the failures of Ricci and De Nobile in India. Later — even well into the twentieth century — it explains the failure of a Father Vincent Lebbe in China. We have, fortunately, reached a turning point with the encyclical *Fidei Donum* of Pius XII (and before him, the great effort in this regard of Benedict XV and Pius XI) along with the document on the missions of Vatican II. We have learned a supremely important lesson here on cultural identification and the faith, but it had to come at a frightful cost to the Church.

The Church must be in a continuously missionary state if it is to be faithful to its evangelical origins. It is a state in which the Church goes outside of herself to confront and dialogue with each culture, with the atheist and as well as the believer, to bring them, as the Holy Spirit gives it to her, the good news of salvation; and to do this, she must both understand and be understood; she must become incarnate herself within the cultural dynamics of each age of man. This "relationship of the Church to the world," this missionary activity to and for the world is an essential dimension of her being in the world. This task cannot be done by simply having the Church construct her own world within another world which would exist "out there," having her own charitable and educational institutions "alongside" or in competition with that of the secular world.

In this way, she fails in her missionary activity understood in its basic ecclesial meaning, she fails to influence the secular world from within as a leaven principle and it is here that we have the very crux of our problem today. It is, in more vulgar terms, nothing more than a continuation of her particularized ghetto which has been hers from the time she first confronted the modern world some 400 years ago. Her answer to this world has been to build an individualistic morality so that each Christian could "save his soul" amid the difficult and complex social reality which encased and crushed him on every side and from which he fled in fear to the comfort and silence of the Church. The Church gave him the consolation he so longed for (legitimate in itself), but neglected the problem of letting the world "outside" develop on its own dynamism. The result, as the history of the modern period abundantly shows, has been a tragic one both for society as well as the Church. This explains also the fact that when the Church in the modern period started its *aggiornamento* in this respect, the Popes' efforts were met with shock and dismay. When Leo XIII published *Rerum Novarum* in 1891, many Christians were scandalized by his words, and some bishops even refused to publish Leo's teachings in their dioceses. Exaggerated individualism and conservatism (ironically called liberalism in the nineteenth century) have traditionally blasted all social reform with bromides and specious arguments about freedom from interference, private rights, private initiative, and the all-pervading "creeping socialism." The ironic truth of the matter is that it is precisely this type of individualistic thinking separated from social consciousness that has led to a "split personality" in Catholic and Christian thinking. It was the abuses of *laissez-faire* politics, for instance, which both necessitated governmental intervention and cleared the way for the opposite error, that of Communism in the nineteenth century. Granted, for instance, that I can do what I please with my property, then naturally I can shift the location of my plant without regard to employee dislocation; I can fire and hire without regard to collective bargaining; I can engage in rack renting, high real estate speculation and in a host of other activities which result in social harm. Discrimination against the Negro, for instance, caps a long list of abuses resulting from the conservative view of the "sanctity" of private property. And, of course, this is only one result of the Christian ghetto mentality vis-à-vis the modern world. Having no real Christian approach to these problems, they have mentally and spiritually taken over the principles of self-aggrandizement and avarice ("social mobility") which constitute an amoral system of thought whereby Christians are led today in the social order.

The Christian community, then, has tended to exist alongside of, not within, the community of the new and revolutionary men of our day. The Church's mission today must be to re-orient her energies for penetration from the within of this beleaguered world such as it is and such as it has become, to humanize and christianize it. This, of course, does not mean that she must now immediately destroy the mass of institutions she has created and which have served her well in the past, incarnating as they once did the evangelical message of love and fraternity in a world which simply had not the means of doing it in any other way. It does mean, however, a new approach and, above all, a corresponding new mentality to and for the world of our day. The temporal institutions in which the Church has incarnated her testimony of love and fraternity will have to be phased out to the proportion and extent that she realizes that it is the whole world which needs her ministrations and this in a most desperate way. And this can only come about by an incarnation of the Church within the constructs of this new world so that she can influence it from within. It is simply self-defeating to her mission, for instance, for her to invest some millions of dollars and, say, the apostolic labors of 300 priests and nuns for 2000 "Catholic" students, whereas down the road there is a secular campus (where the ideas that guide society really develop) with 25,000 students (10,000 Catholics at that) who have two "chaplains." This is simply a failure in evangelical witness of the Church, and it can be gainsaid by no argument "for" Catholic schools.

All this will require an emphasis away from separation and ghettoism and independent constructs to that of service of the world within the world as it exists in our day. The day must certainly come — the sooner the better for the Church's mission — when we will no longer need the crutches of parallel institutions, separate hospitals, schools, charities, etc., but this will come about only to the degree that the Church shall have shifted its view from constructing her own world to that of service in helping to construct in a human and Christian manner the secular world of the twentieth century. The modern world in which we live is a profane and desacralized world and it is within this world that the Christian must give testimony to the Word of God. It is no longer a crusade "against" or a vulgar proselytism to "win the world," but a loving presence, an influencing presence within the world for good. This "sacrament" of the Christian's presence, active and incarnational, must become the chief focal point around which any theology of the Church in the world can be built as the Church prepares for entrance into the new post-Constantinian age of renewal.

VII

If what we have said above is true, then it ought to be evident that a new approach to the problems of the modern world is an absolute imperative. Religion in general and Christianity in particular, as it stands today at least, are not taken seriously in effecting any major change in the life of our times. Christianity is simply deemed irrelevant to questions of war and peace, of the economy, of evolving nations, of freedom, etc. There are many things which must be done and in a schematic way these can be reduced to four:

1) We must establish a moral order for people on a new level of freedom and sophistication to meet the highly technical problems of our day.

2) We must reach a new depth of the mortal mystery of the human condition of the Church so as to curtail the pompous pretension of ecclesiastical conceit. The humility and service concept of the Church must replace all the rhetoric and apologetic of triumphalism, still with us from a former age.

3) We must, as did Vatican II as a beginning in the *Constitution on the Liturgy*, give worship a boldness and spontaneity so that people can express themselves vigorously and joyously in modes and language that they understand.

4) We must work for a depth of faith which will give birth to an unlimited compassion and love for the human family, which was not viewed sympathetically by traditional parochial limits and piety. The whole world, in other words, with its problems and agonies, must become our parish.

These, of course, are the most generalized problems which confront the Church in an age of renewal. There are more specific ones which must be touched on if we are to make our survey more complete and concrete. These could be reduced to four and we can only lightly touch upon them; formulization, poverty, dialogue, and the theology of temporal accomplishments.

1) The first problem is one of communication with the modern world in getting it first to understand what we are talking about.

It is a question of the cultural transformation of the very formulization of Christian truths to meet the challenge of today. Pope John touched on this basic problem in his opening talk to the fathers of Vatican II. It will have to be done at first on a sort of trial and error basis, for we simply do not know what formulizations can or cannot be made to serve Christian truth, which formulizations are or are not intelligible to modern men. There will be some errors here, as perhaps happened in the attempt to substitute "transignification" for "transubstantiation," but at least some effort was made to meet this great problem head on. Even the encyclical *Mysterium Fidei* of Paul VI recognized the problem and encouraged theologians to develop thought along these lines.

2) The second great problem of the Church in the modern world is that of poverty in the two-thirds of the world undergoing most rapid development today. Blindness of heart will find no forgiveness either here or in the next world. The poor, in a sense, are God's gift to Western man, a last appeal to salvation to a portion of mankind grown fat and selfish in its superabundance, and absolutely blind to the evangelical message of poverty and service so necessary for salvation.

But the Council's words are also words of hope: hope to affluent Christians that there is still time to see Christ in the millions of the world's poor before their hearts are shut off from salvation by this blindness to the poor; hope to the world's poor as well, by reminding all men that each is his brother's keeper and that, in the words of John XXIII, "We are all responsible for the poor of the world" (*Mater et Magistra*). Hope, too, that what is impossible to man is possible to God, that the words of the Holy Spirit addressed to all men through the Council Fathers will penetrate the hardening hearts of many Western Christians.

This doctrine of evangelical poverty is part and parcel of practically every text of the New Testament. Jesus, during his short stay on this earth, deliberately chose to be poor, lived with the poor, and showed preferential love to the poor. They were His constant companions, and the spirit and reality of poverty would be one of the main characteristics of His kingdom. The Gospel texts establishing this truth are so numerous that it would simply be impossible to cite them all.

Jesus Christ was born poor, lived poor, and died a poor man's death. He was born in a manger (Lk 2:7); the offering given at His presentation was that of the poor (Lk 2:24); He was known and even disparagingly referred to as "the son of a carpenter" (Mt 13:15); He claimed no permanent abode while performing His public ministry (Mt 8:20); His death was that of a poor, naked, and crucified criminal (Jn 19:23); He was even buried in the tomb of another man (Mt 27:59).

The preferential love which Christ had for the poor is proverbial throughout the evangelical texts. The bulk of His ministry was spent among the most despised of men of the society of His time. The first to be told of His birth were poor shepherds (Lk 2:8); His disciples were fishermen, a poor class (Mt 4:18); His love for the multitude was spontaneous and affective (Mt 9:35; 10:3); one of the signs of His mission was that He had been sent to preach the Gospel to the poor (Lk 4:8); many times He openly defended the cause of the poor (Lk 16:19; Mk 13:41); Christ continuously identified Himself with the poor (Mt 25:31); He had some very harsh words for the rich who were selfish with their wealth (Lk 6:24).

The importance of poverty for every man who wishes to enter His kingdom is fundamental in the Sermon on the Mount. Poverty of spirit and of fact is listed first in all the evangelists. Nor was His proclamation of poverty restricted to "spiritual" poverty, it must tend to express and incarnate itself in actual *de facto* poverty. In this way, Christ was clearly teaching that the spirit of poverty (once again that paradox) enables us to realize the blessedness of material poverty, and that such a spirit is more easily attainable when one is materially poor than when one lives in the midst of riches. Thus He proclaims the poor to be blessed (Lk 6:20). The service of Mammon is opposed to that of God (Mt 6:24); He severely rebuked those who strive only after material goods (Mt 6:30). He warned against riches, which tend to choke the Word of God (Mt 13:22); material possessions are only of a very temporal nature (Lk 12:13; Mt 6:19); He proclaimed that detachment is a necessary element of Christian perfection (Mt 19:16; Lk 14:33). He continuously reminds us how difficult it really is for the rich to work out their salvation (Mt 16:22). Christ promises great rewards for those who renounce earthly goods for the sake of the kingdom (Mt 19:27). Above all, as an example to the rest of the faithful, He commands His apostles to be poor in the exercise of their mission and ministry (Lk 9:3).

The teachings of Christ on poverty, both in word and example, are astounding and even scandalous, except to him to whom God has given the grace. In the sick world of the materialistic and selfish twentieth century, this doctrine appears once again to be the "stupidity" and "stumbling block" which St. Paul noted in his First Epistle to the Corinthians. But with this twist: it is a "stupidity" to many who bear the name of Christian in the midst of plenty.

Yet the Church is the living continuation in space and time of the mystery of Jesus Christ. It must therefore show forth in its words and actions the very poverty of its Lord and Master as well as its deep solicitude for the poor and rejected of this earth. In the words of Pope Paul VI: "The poor are the image of Christ, even a living sacrament, as it were." Thus the Church must be renewed to restore its pristine, evangelical message of poverty to the world. That is why Pope John could say that Vatican II, in its efforts to "restore to the visage of the Church the same resplendence of purity and simplicity which characterized her at the beginning," is providing an exceptional opportunity for the Church to rid herself of all that actually impedes her from being, in the eyes of the world, poor like Jesus Christ.

The Church must manifest her preferential love for the poor in concrete ways in order to benefit the great masses of poor all over the globe. The world today expects more from the Church than mere expressions of love or enunciations of general principles; it asks for tangible and concrete proof of this love. The whole Church, from bishops to laymen, must take a stand, clearly and courageously, in favor of the poor every time they are victims of any injustice. This evidently implies a more forceful stand on racial discrimination, medical aid for the aged, urban renewal in all of its forms. Thus her solicitude for social justice in concrete examples will become a proof of her love for the poor. She must rebuke public authorities when they fail in their obligations to take necessary measures to solve or alleviate the most urgent social problems of the day.

The Church must continuously remind herself and all men that the rich have no special claims among the people of God, except that they have been given a special obligation, by virtue of their wealth, to be servants of God's poor. They themselves must be poor in spirit, in the above-mentioned sense, and this attitude should characterize all of their actions. The Church has a heavy responsibility to remind the rich that unless they are poor at least in this sense, their chances for salvation are very slim indeed. The poor belong to the Church in their own right, as born citizens of God's kingdom, who have a first claim to His mercy and love. In the Church of God, they have the primacy of honor. The Church must always uphold this hierarchy of spiritual values, not only because her Divine Founder did so before her, but also to neutralize the idolatry of riches which in so many ways dominates modern society.

It is true that even if the Church should offer all this testimony to poverty and to her predilection for the poor, to her exalting the virtue of poverty, the world will not immediately come to believe in Christ and receive the good news of salvation. But at least the Church will have been able to surmount one of the greatest obstacles which prevents so many people from recognizing her as the body of Christ, as the continuation of the mystery of the poor man of Galilee. She will thus render the way to faith easier for those who seek this evangelical testimony as the indispensable credential of the true Church of Jesus Christ. The Church, if genuinely and really poor, will be the best proclamation of Christ to the world. Without it, we can forget about *aggiornamento* and continue to emphasize a defunct apologetics from which many men of good will turn away, shocked and scandalized. They wish to see Christ, and what we continue to give them is cold, rational argument.

The poor man is Christ, and if the Christian cannot come to see Christ in him, he will never see Christ, either here below or in the future life. "Depart from me . . . . for if you have not done it to one of these the least of my brothers, you have not done it to me" (Mt 25:26); to the man of the world, the enemy is he who would threaten his social status, his economic prosperity, his racial caste, his absolute license to do what he wants with no interference from men or the state. This enemy is the conspirator, the enemy from within and from without, the subversive of "cultural" and religious" values who must be destroyed at all costs; the Christian seeks out his enemy to do him good, to return benevolence for malevolence, who seeks what binds and heals rather than what separates and destroys; who knows that even when he must resist the injustices of his enemy there are bounds of morality beyond which he may not go and who must never discontinue the sometimes discouraging attempt to seek peace and an atmosphere of trust and confidence. For his pains, furthermore, the Christian must be prepared, like Jeremiah of long ago, to himself be considered a "traitor" or "soft" on a hated group or at best a subversive whose motives will lead to "surrender" and "destruction."

Thus, some paradoxes of the Christian will only inspire a smile or a shrug from the man of the world. He will consider the Christian stupid in the Pauline sense of this word (1 Cor 2:8) or at best a crackpot preacher of doom who must be tolerated in a "liberal" and "free" society. Other paradoxes will inspire in the man of the world rage and active opposition. This is nothing new; Stephen was the prototype in Acts 6:8, and today this hatred is directed against those "softhearts" who seek nuclear disarmament, racial justice, a genuine international society, protection for migrant workers and for the aged.

American Catholics, Father Edward Duff, S.J., has reminded us, were deeply troubled by the thesis of Rolf Hochhuth's *The Deputy;* they were disturbed by the accusation of Guenter Lewy's book that the Church in Germany failed to face up to moral evil, failed to look beyond its institutional interests. Will future generations accuse us of preoccupation with magnificent building programs to the point of hideous insensitivity to the brutal hunger, misery, and ignorance of countless millions of our fellow human beings throughout the globe? Our preoccupation with such building programs must seem a mockery of Christian commitment when we look out of our institutional walls just for a second to see a billion and a half human beings go to bed hungry every single night of God's holy year. When we view such a scandal, is it any wonder that we believing Christians need honesty and courage in admitting our own responsibility for the thundering advance of atheism in a world in which for two thousand years the Gospel has been preached. It is because our individual and collective conduct as Christians has so seldom conformed to the evangelical spirit of poverty that whole masses of the world's population look away from Christianity in disgust and horror. When they witness the sickening spectacle of a Congress of this "Christian nation" cutting to pieces a miserable two-billion-dollar foreign aid bill, which would provide economic and technical assistance to millions of their fellowmen, while these same comfortable Christians idly sit back to enjoy a GNP of over 660 billion dollars, it is no wonder that atheism is on the increase all over this great land of ours. Even at home, the forty million poor Americans must accept a miserable 900 million dollars as crumbs from the hands of the rich in an anti-poverty bill.

In this context, the words of Vatican II on poverty come as both a warning and a hope. They are a warning to the affluent Christians in many countries of the world, who must henceforth understand very clearly the Christian meaning of wealth and riches. If a Christian has wealth, he must use it in the service of the brothers who are poor and in need. The Gospel is very blunt here: only by sharing, only by giving of himself and his wealth can the rich Christian hope to escape the clear condemnations of many of the gospel texts. The Council's words are an appeal to return to this evangelical poverty of spirit and in fact which is essential for entrance into the kingdom of God. The tendency to materialism is one of the foremost dangers of the Western world; concomitant with this pragmatic materialism is apathy and unconcern toward the poor.

3) Our third great modern problem today for the Church is that of dialogue, particularly with the atheistic and communistic world of our day. It will do no good to continue the long repertoire of condemnations — which have failed to either stop or solve the problem. Only a bold confrontation and dialogue can offer hope of fruitfulness here. We shall develop this aspect later in our study.

4) Our final problem will have to deal with a theology of the direction and accomplishments of the new industrial-technical world in which we live. The proper spirituality of the layman and his sanctification must be sought in fulfilling that specific work which is his. In other words, his proper function is the incarnation of the divine life into the temporal domain, and in fulfilling this work he will reach his own spiritual goal. With the eyes of faith (for faith is nothing more than God's vision of all reality, celestial and terrestrial, engrafted onto ours) he must fully enter into the temporal in all of its ramifications to bring out the image of God. Man is God's lieutenant in creation, prolonging creation according to the image of God and man given to him in faith. His proper mortification will be to purify continuously his own intentions and not to be perturbed that, at times, he sees no direct connection between his work and the kingdom, the supernatural as such. If faith is demanded in God's mysteries, so too is faith required for the restoring of the temporal order to God, for we do not fully understand all of its ramifications and consequences. But one thing is and must remain certain for him in his research, in his laboratory, at his machine, at his microscope, in his struggle for just laws and social justice, on his tractor on an American farm or in an undeveloped country: the layman

is doing God's will in prolonging creation and fulfilling his proper apostolate in the Church of God. In this sense, the layman partakes of the work of the Church in its full and cosmic sense.

The problem of the relationship between theology and technology is more complicated. But at least we can say a few things as to its meaning and orientation for the Christian.

The terms "science" and "technology" are certainly not the same. Science is habitually used in a much broader sense to include all of the pure and applied sciences while technology is used almost exclusively to mean the practical applied sciences alone. In our present context, the two terms are used indiscriminately since the so-called "common man," when he speaks of them, means the same thing.

This problem more than any other is peculiar to modern man. The development in the sciences during the past 200 years has far outstripped the combined advances of mankind in all previous history. It has affected man not only in a quantitative measure (more facility of travel, better conditions, etc.) but to an even larger degree in a qualitative measure. Four main observations, we believe, are in order with regard to the qualitative effects of technology.

1) With the more perfect technology developed over the space of recent years, servile work ("slavery" to work as some theologians call it) has become constantly reduced. Man is no longer the slave to nature's whims (draughts, floods, insects, etc.) in his efforts to transform nature. Science has thus permitted the more spiritual aspects of man to develop freely, if not always *de facto*, since, even here, men reserve their option of free will.

2) Through the advance of the social sciences, it has become more and more possible to regulate as well as dominate the course of social events: "socialization" at its best in its moderate forms (cf. *Mater et Magistra*), organization of insurances, unemployment benefits, just distribution of quantitative taxes, etc. This aspect of the social sciences is an indispensable factor in making the benefits of technology accessible to the great majority of the people in a particular civilization.

3) Augmentation of productivity permits modern civilization to work effectively and with a definite method for the suppression of enormous inequalities, both economic and social. The possibility is at our disposal to eliminate or at least to alleviate to a large degree the so-called "underdeveloped" countries of the world. Never before in history has this possibility been ours. Pius XII and John XXIII have pointed out the fact that most nations have the possibility of self-sufficiency if they can only develop and evenly distribute their enormous, untouched resources. We, of the West, with our superior technological advances are in a position to aid them. This indeed is one of the great dramas of our time, technology and economic development.

4) As a result of the above, for the first time in history all men can truly collaborate in mastering nature and in advancing truly human goals. The future generations as well as the present must turn their thoughts from a narrow nationalism, self-centered history, and concern to the international (interplanetary) scene more and more. "International responsibility" is no longer a high-sounding moral phrase; it is a definitive fact already acquired in certain realms (think of the U.N. and the great work of its subsidiary organizations, such as UNESCO, WHO, etc.). Technology has brought about the era of a humanity which is truly and effectively universal. A common life in which all share has made us more and more a cosmopolitan and even cosmic civilization.

One cannot, however, deny the inherent drawbacks of technology and science as we know them today. These difficulties are cited because they continue to cause much worry to Catholic thinkers on this subject, almost to the point of obsessions. Witness, for example, the rather negative approach to this problem by a symposium recently carried on under the auspices of the Catholic University of America: "Technology and the Christian." Let us observe that:

1) It does not automatically follow that technological progress necessarily means a perfection of man. It can help by liberating man from the slavery of want, disease, but at the same time can

lead to a dissipation of leisure time in meaningless activity that is so common among Americans.

2) Technology and science in a sense are, in the words of Reinhold Niebuhr, ambiguous in themselves. They can be used for great good (think of the tremendous good which could come from the Telstar) or turned to great evil (think of Hiroshima, etc.). Unless Christians attempt to influence the current of thought along the lines of good, there is little hope that any satisfactory solution will be found.

3) Such a progress easily leads to materialism. What was done before by prayer is done now by medicine. "Religion is the opium of the people." Much Christian thinking has given the enemy occasion for such accusation. The true Christian thinker versed in both religion and technology can serve to prove the great lie of their incompatibility. There is indeed great need of a modern apologetic.

4) Our society has tended to make men strangers to each other and slaves to the technological system (one thinks here as the organization man). More thought must be given to this problem by the theologians and sociologists alike.

And, finally, cannot the progress of science and technology itself be a liberating force for man, a prefiguration or prelude of the coming of the kingdom? Cannot international trade agreements serve as foretastes of the harmony, peace, and, above all, of the fraternal love in sharing, as a figure of spiritual goods, the material goods necessary for a decent human existence? And cannot there be a definitive theological interpretation of automation (with all its drawbacks) as a means whereby man is freed to perform more human tasks, work more in conformity with his noble vocation as artifex, impregnating matter and leading it toward what it will be definitively under the supreme eschatological work of the great Artifex who is Christ? Here is what even a man of the world, G. Piel, has to say about this:

> The liberation of people from tasks unworthy of human capacity should free that capacity for a host of activities now neglected in our civilization: teaching and learning — funda-

> mental scientific investigation, the performing arts and graphic arts, letters, the crafts, politics and social science. Characteristically these activities involve the interaction of people rather than things (*Consumers of Abundance*, p. 9).

Certainly, we cannot eliminate the cross from this perhaps too optimistic view of the elaboration of the temporal order under the inspiration of the Holy Spirit. The historical sequence is not always a forward-moving sequence; it has its backslidings, its failures, its drawbacks; but the Christian should not, and must not, become discouraged. Perhaps these very setbacks will be an occasion, providential perhaps, the purification of intention, renewal of purpose, and dedication for Christ and for men, *instaurare omnia in Christo*. In the wise words of Father Thils:

> But if we have faith in the total efficacy (supernatural and natural) of the Spirit, if we believe that God is more powerful than Satan, if we admit that the grace of Christ is more abundant than the sin of Adam, we can estimate that the weight of good realized in the world by the Holy Spirit will be dominant, that it will even grow without suppressing the reactions and oppositions of man and the devil, taking the ensemble of men, by ways and detours, toward a greater peace, more liberty, and even greater sanctity (*Théologie et réalité Sociale*, p. 300).

CHAPTER II

PRIVATE PROPERTY, CAPITALISM, AND JOHN XXIII*

* Reprinted with the permission of the editor from the April, 1966 issue of *Social Digest*. The comments of Father Hubert F. Schiffer, S.J., editor of *Social Digest* are of interest. He notes:

Speaking as a professional economist, I must confess that I am not too happy about some of the author's sweeping assumptions. Sure enough, he is right in his strong condemnation of the capitalist system. But the old, classical capitalism is quite dead today, isn't it? At least in the U. S. and most of the economically developed countries, we are living in a "private enterprise system" that is far removed from pure Capitalism with its ruthless individualism and its complete lack of government regulations. Instead, our corporate profit taxes take almost one-half of profits and use them for the common good. Unemployment, health, accident, and life insurance form part of our system; industrial pension plans are widespread. All these forms of social security and other "fringe benefits" bring steadily increasing advantages to employees, in addition to their wages and salaries. We have costly industrial training programs, company paid scholarships, and the like. It is estimated that approximately 120,000 companies have various profit-sharing plans for their employees; while this number is relatively small in comparison to the total number of U. S. firms, it does include some very large corporations. Does all this sound like the old-style capitalism of the nineteenth century where the profit motive was the only guide?

In many underdeveloped countries, of course, the situation is quite different. There, it is true, classical capitalism is still rampant in too many cases.

Despite these reservations, however, I am happy that Father Riga has touched on several important points that merit serious consideration. One of them is the need for a more widely diffused ownership of property in modern society — productive property, not only consumer goods. The author's observation that we do have political democracy, but not economic democracy, is quite correct. Political democracy is highly praised as a sign of progress and maturity. Why, then, is economic democracy so often attacked as dangerous? If the community of work is to be more than a pious platitude uttered at business luncheons, should not all the participants in the productive process — including the employees — be encouraged to exercise some responsibility and have some representative voice in the management of their companies? Why should this representation be limited to those who invest their money and be denied to those who invest a lifetime of work?

Sure enough, we have labor unions — some of them not very influential, and some too powerful — but only slightly more than one out of every five people in the U. S. labor force belongs to any kind of labor union. And the "suggestion box" is clearly not the most effective way to elicit a true cooperative effort. What can be done? That's where creative thinking comes in. . . . With this, dear reader, I mean YOU!

Who can deny that the gigantic size of many modern corporations and their "*urge to merge*" (as *Fortune* magazine puts it) create a whole slew of new social problems? A new mercantilism of government ownership of these ever-expanding giant corporations can hardly be the answer, because the government should govern and not run businesses, but the present trends toward "diversification" are creating grave dangers of economic dictatorship. . . .

One final word about the profit motive. There, it seems to me, the author is needlessly harsh, without the necessary distinctions. What is wrong with profits? And what is wrong with hoping for profits? I don't see why the profit motive should necessarily *destroy the community of work* and be dehumanizing — unless it is the one and only motive, "using" people for material gain. Profit for profit's sake *is* dehumanizing, but can the term "profit motive" be limited, arbitrarily, to that one narrow meaning? If an enterprise provides a service to the community by helping to increase its living standards, if it provides employment and pays a fair share of its income in wages and fringe benefits, why shouldn't the profit motive also be included in the overall picture? Isn't this what many responsible businessmen of today are trying to accomplish? Compared to their efforts and successes, the employment policies and wages of many Church-related institutions are abominable indeed.

In the following pages we wish to treat of capitalism as a regime, as an institution long since established in the West (above all in the United States) and not necessarily of individual capitalists who, as we shall show, are together with the workers caught up in the inexorable process of capitalization which has its own laws and orientations. Neither proprietors nor workers can, of themselves, control the system of capitalism itself since they are both caught up in its circle of inhumanity. We define the system of capitalism as one of an ownership of the means of production (capital) by some (individual or group), while others who are not proprietors are employed to produce goods by means of these capital investments. Such a system of itself and in itself has never been condemned by the Church and from a theoretical point of view has found some approval in pontifical documents. Pius XI gave a very balanced view in this respect in his encyclical *Quadragesimo Anno*. He balances out very neatly the public (social) function of property and means of production with the corresponding right to ownership (individual), thus summing up the teachings of Leo XIII:

> First, let it be made clear beyond all doubt that neither Leo XIII, nor those theologians who have taught under the guidance and direction of the Church, had ever denied or called in question the two-fold aspect of ownership, which is individual or social according as it regards individuals or concerns the common good. Their unanimous assertion has always been that the right to own private property has been given to man by nature, or rather by the Creator Himself, both in order that individuals may be able to provide for their own needs and those of their families, and also that by means of it the goods which the Creator has destined for the whole human race may truly serve this purpose. Now these ends cannot be secured, unless some definite and stable order is maintained.
>
> A double danger must therefore be carefully avoided, on the one hand, if the social and public aspect of ownership be denied or minimized, one falls into "individualism," as it is called, or at least comes near to it; on the other hand, the rejection or diminution of its private and individual character necessarily leads to "collectivism" or to something approaching to it (par. 45).

We shall see later how John XXIII will expand this notion. This system, however, as every other temporal expression of man's personality in space and in time, must be continuously evaluated and re-examined in the light of humanizing and christianizing principles to see if it has deviated from its proper end: the promotion of the dignity of the men involved in the institution or enterprise along with its effects on the human community in which it exists. For this major principle of social philosophy is the sole legitimate one for any Christian examining the social order in a moral context. John XXIII never tired of repeating this throughout his life. For a random sampling see *Mater et Magistra* (pars. 18, 21, 55, 62, 74, 91, 106–107, 125, 142, 149, 157, 209, etc.) and *Pacem in Terris* (pars. 9–18, 20, 24, 26, 28, 34, 41, 44, 47, 65, 73, 79, 139, etc.). This is the foundation of the whole teaching of the Church on the social order. It is important also that we emphasize this organizational-institutional aspect of the capitalist system since for too many Christians in the West — so long versed in a condemnation of the communistic system — the capitalist system has, by some sort of default, been given express or implicit approval by the Church. This is disastrous for, as we shall hope to show, the capitalist system, being vitiated at its very root, must also be condemned by the Christian as inhuman and demoralizing, as any history of nineteenth-century industrialism or its effects on the twentieth century will clearly show.

Thus it is the structure of capitalism itself which we must investigate to see if it does in fact meet the unique criterion for morality, namely, that of promotion of the human person. This is doubly important today in a period of a highly developed social system, where (as we shall see further in our study) the socialization of modern life has become the vital milieu in which men live and which, for better or worse, has immense influence on the individual who lives and works with such a socialized structure. The distress in the economic and social sphere on both a national and above all on an international scale is not dependent on any particular individual or individuals, but on a whole system of capital which runs its own course with its own laws and which can be cured only at its root cause: personalizing what has been brutally and inhumanly depersonalized in this system; the distress proceeds from a profoundly dislocated social and economic structure in the East (communism) and in the West (capitalism). It is for that reason that both systems have had inhuman effects on the human person; the individual is caught up in the system on both sides of the iron-dollar curtain: both systems reduce the human person to a means for economic progress — communism, by putting him at the complete service of the state and progress of the community, and capitalism, by using the human person in its all engulfing profit motive. Therefore, both of them must be condemned by Christian morality. The popes have not been remiss in this task, even if it seems that their condemnations of the communist system have been enunciated more often. The difference between Eastern Communism in practice and Western Capitalism in practice is only an apparent one.

I. BASIC IDEAS

At first glance, the profit motive system, which is at the base of capitalism, is one of the most natural things in the world. It is rather elementary economics. A man buys a product and seeks to resell it at a higher price and cost than what he paid for it by performance of a service for the public (we presuppose that things like taxes, overhead, etc., have all been reduced from his gross profit). The rationale is that such a return will permit him to make a living for himself and his family by reason of his service as intermediary or producer which he performs for the public. He thus acts in a system of supply and demand as an intermediary to fulfill a public and social service for others. Thus an honest profit can accrue to him who fulfills such a public function which in its own turn — precisely because it is a public and social act — can be morally and in fact legally regulated by the public authority for the common good of its citizens who are not always able to regulate these things themselves, by means of laws (e.g., food and drug laws) and by taxes (personal, corporative, and hidden). The benefits of profit can be more or less altered for the common good but not so much that it will effectively crush the personal initiative of the citizens. It is this social destiny of goods and services which gives a government the legal and moral right to intervene in the economy of a nation. Pope John pointed this out many times, as did his predecessors. Because of the vastness, power, and complexity of modern economy, the state has a positive right to intervene authoritatively to insure justice in all sectors of economic affairs. Repeating Leo XIII, John XXIII says in *Mater et Magistra:*

> The state, whose very reason for existence is the realization of the common good in the temporal order, cannot keep aloof from the economy. It should be present to promote in a suitable manner the production of a sufficient supply of material goods, the use of which is necessary for the practice of virtue, and to watch over the rights of all citizens, especially of the weaker among them, such as workers, women, and children. It has also the inflexible duty of contributing actively to the betterment of the workers' standard of living (par 20).

The novelty of Pope John's teaching is that this principle is further extended. If the state had the right to intervene in economic and social matters in 1891, when society was not so complicated and developed as it is today, this right must apply with greater force now. State influence and intervention must necessarily be more extended today because the economy on a national and an international scale has become more vast and complicated.

In his discussion, the Pope maintains a balanced position between two extremes: those who would deny, as much as possible, any state regulatory activity in the economy, considering its necessity a lesser of two evils; and those who would permit the government to regulate or control the whole economic process by various types of socialism. For Pope John, intervention by the state is not an evil; rather, the state has a positive moral duty to maintain distributive justice in any given society and economy. State intervention, however, must not destroy the private initiative of the citizens; it must promote and safeguard it. This delicate balance is what the popes have called *the principle of subsidiarity:* that is, the state helps or takes over for private groups and individuals only when they cannot do it themselves. Pope John reasons as follows:

> At the outset it should be affirmed that in economic affairs first place is to be given to the private initiative of individual men who, either working by themselves, or with others in one fashion or another, pursue their common interests (par. 51).
>
> This intervention of public authorities that encourages, stimulates, regulates, supplements, and complements, is based on the principle of subsidiarity as set forth by Pius XI in the encyclical *Quadragesimo Anno*: "It is a fundamental principle of social philosophy, fixed and unchangeable, that one should not withdraw from individuals and commit to the community what they can accomplish by their own enterprise and industry. So, too, it is an injustice and at the same time a grave evil and a disturbance of the right order, to transfer to the larger and higher organization functions which can be performed and provided for by lesser and subordinate bodies. Inasmuch as every social activity should, by its very nature, prove a help to members of the body social, it should never destroy or absorb them" (par. 53).

Thus, the state's whole reason for existence is to be of service to the human person, promoting his progress and dignity. From the very beginning, the personalistic tone of this letter is evident. The state exists for the person, not the person for the state; the state intervenes in the social order to promote and safeguard human values, not to suppress them.

Ultimately, state intervention has a profound human meaning which was also brought out in *Pacem in Terris* (par. 65–66.). Each human person has a natural right to develop his talents, and he must do this of his own free will. In *Quadragesimo Anno*, Pope Pius XI capsulized this concept in the principle of subsidiarity; a society may not appropriate to itself the initiative which can be assumed by the individual. The foundation of this principle lies in the irreplaceable value of a person's free initiative in directing his destiny. Since each person must fulfill his own destiny through his own genius, he must be able to take advantage of all the means necessary to develop it. The function of the public authority is simply to create favorable conditions for this development.

The Pope also brings out the social reason that underpins the principle of subsidiarity: the riches and fruitfulness of society come from the diversity of its members, and this diversity is obviously related to the way in which each person develops his individual talents. The fullest exercise of human rights occurs when the individual's will keeps pace with his ability, and when his ability is confined by nothing but its own limitations. As this diversity is allowed to develop, society is enriched. That form of society then, which permits and encourages each of its members to perfect his potential, perfects itself, and by that very fact it becomes more personalistic in its conception of man. The Pope seems never to tire of drawing our attention to this personalism which must be evinced by any just social order.

> The doctrine that has been set forth above obviously does not prohibit the state and other public agencies from lawfully possessing productive goods, particularly when they carry with them an opportunity for domination that is so great that it cannot be left in the hands of private individuals without injury to the community at large (par. 116).
>
> It seems characteristic of our times to vest more and more ownership of goods in the state and in other public bodies. This is partially explained by the fact that the common good requires public authorities to exercise ever greater responsibilities. However, in this matter, the principle of subsidiarity, already mentioned above, is to be strictly observed. For it is lawful for states and public corporations to expand their domain of ownership only when manifest and genuine requirements of the common good so require, and then with safeguards, lest the possession of private citizens be diminished beyond measure, or, what is worse, destroyed (par. 117).

Governments, notes the Pope, have gained immense knowledge about depressions and "slump" periods. Their experience in the past, especially during the 1930's, has shown them how to counter slumps: easy money, tax cuts, easy credit, stepped-up spending, international cooperation on trade, and other measures. In the United States, there are legal safeguards against depressions through the Employment Act of 1946.

BALANCE BETWEEN PUBLIC AND PRIVATE EFFORTS

In underdeveloped countries, intervention by the state will obviously be greater than in those countries which are more highly developed economically. In order that each sector of the economy — agriculture, industry, and services — may develop in a balanced relationship to every other sector, the Pope gives his full approval to government planning and regulation of the economy (par. 151). Yet this is but a temporary measure; and as soon as possible, or as soon as the common good permits it, private citizens and "intermediary bodies" ought to be allowed to take over (par. 152). The ideal situation is that public and private elements of the country work together for the common good. A balance must be maintained between the two, for a destruction of one by the other is immoral and contrary to the common good. When either of the two gains the ascendancy, an absolutist social structure develops which is always harmful to the total well-being of society. In other words, society is be seen as a total body which is kept balanced by the mutual cooperation of private and public enterprise.

> Experience, in fact, shows that where the personal initiative of individuals is lacking, political tyranny appears. Moreover, stagnation occurs in a number of areas of the economy, and shortages are felt in a wide variety of consumer goods and services of a kind designed not only to meet material wants, but more particularly to satisfy needs of the spirit, and which thus call into play in a special manner the creative talents of individuals (par. 57).

> Where the state fails to act in economic affairs when it should, or acts defectively, incurable civil disorders are seen to follow. Likewise, unscrupulous men of power — whose breed, alas, grows in every age and place like cockle among the wheat — take advantage of the weak for their own wicked gain (par. 58).

Thus, we can immediately see that from a moral point of view, there is nothing "*essential*" or "*natural*" about the capitalist profit motive system, since, in the natural order, the whole *raison d'être* is the service it renders the common good from which it legitimately and morally earns a "*profit*" in so doing. In the case of true necessity (which Socialists would opt for in our present age of complexification) for the common good, any particular industry or whole complex of industries can be taken over by the public authority and subtracted from the profit enterprise. This is true today in all Western countries in the domain of roads, waterways, heavy industries such as steel, electricity, transportation, etc., all of which, for the most part, were part of the revenues in times past of the king or baron. This process might well have to increase in the future because of the complex interplay of the socialization of modern economy if the public is going to be served in an efficient and less costly manner. This, of course, brings us to the whole question of socialism and socialization as treated by John XXIII.

"SOCIALIZATION"

The appearance of the term "*socialization*" in the English translation of *Mater et Magistra* caused great consternation in Catholic and non-Catholic circles. The reason for this dismay, however, is merely a too hasty reading of the text and the apparent but false connotations of the term. As such, the term socialization does not appear in the Latin text, but it does appear in all modern language editions of the encyclical which were published on the same day as the Latin. Interestingly enough, the Italian text was undoubtedly the Pope's original, and the one which must be compared with the Latin for clarification. Like all other modern language texts, the Italian contained the word "*socialization.*" The problem that the word poses does not necessitate any detailed analysis of the question of translation: it should simply be made clear at the outset that the term socialization does not mean socialism, and that the concept of socialization is an important key to understanding *Mater et Magistra*.

Pope John uses the term socialization in the sense that modern sociologists use it, namely, as a type of global and universal interaction of persons and of things. The concept involves a complicated intertwining of many and varied relationships in the economic, social and technological fields. Since these impersonal relationships affect all nations and peoples, men have become socially dependent on each other in a great number of institutions and associations. This dependency manifests itself in many ways in each of these fields, especially in the economic and industrial complex. These relations are what might be called elements of fact which have united mankind in a unity never before thought possible.

The Pope puts it clearly when he specifies the three fields of politics, economy, and culture. In connection with the process of socialization, he states:

> A glance at the field of science, technology, and economics reveals the following recent developments: the discovery of nuclear energy, its use in the first place for military purposes and now its increasing employment for peaceful ends; the unlimited possibilities opened up by chemistry in the production of synthetic goods; the wider use of machinery and automation in the areas of manufacturing and services; the modernization of agriculture; the virtual annihilation of the distances separating peoples by the new communications media, especially radio and television; the increased speed in all modes of transportation; and the initial conquests of interplanetary space (par. 47).
>
> If we turn our attention to the social field, we see the following developments: the formation of systems of social insurance and, in some more economically advanced states, the introduction of comprehensive social security systems; in labor unions the formation of, and increasing stress on, an attitude of responsibility toward major socio-economic problems; a progressive improvement of basic education; an ever wider distribution of welfare benefits; increased social mobility with a consequent lessening of class distinctions; a greater interest in world events on the part of those with an average education.
>
> Furthermore, the increased efficiency of economic systems in a growing number of states underscores the lack of socio-economic balance between agriculture on the one hand and manufacturing and services on the other; between economically developed and less developed areas within individual states; and, on a world-wide plane, the even more pronounced socio-economic inequalities among nations of different economic advantage (par. 48).

> Similarly, when one examines the political field, a host of innovations come to light: in many states, a participation in public life by an increasing number of citizens from different social strata; more frequent and extensive intervention by public authorities in the economic and social fields. To these developments must be added, on the international level, the passing of colonial regimes and the attainment of political independence by the peoples of Asia and Africa; the increase of close relations between peoples and a deepening of their interdependence; the emergence and development of a supranational network of organizations having a world-wide scope and pursuing economic, social, cultural or common political ends (par. 49).

WORLDWIDE INTERDEPENDENCE

Communication relays in space make possible an almost instantaneous reporting of news in every part of the globe. Because the world's economic life has become interdependent through a more diversified demand for goods and raw materials, countries today must plan their economic life in relation to that of other countries. Science and technology have become international endeavors with no national boundaries. Culture itself is becoming worldwide. While each country retains and develops its proper genius, it is enriched by absorbing various elements from other cultures. All of these technological, economic, and cultural changes have been of great service in advancing civilization, that is, a greater sharing, on a global basis, of the common patrimony of all men by all men. History never before knew anything like this intensification which began with the Industrial Revolution and has been continuing at a breathtaking pace.

Yet, while these changes have had a profound influence on the social life of modern man, they can also have some stultifying effects on the free initiative and liberty of man. Pope John does not hesitate to give his recommendations to avoid the disadvantages of this modern phenomenon.

There are two ways in which the dangers of rapid change can be avoided. First, the Pope encourages the establishment and growth of intermediary groups and bodies which will assume the freedom of initiative, and which, as a result, will be conducive to the freedom of individuals. The value of these particular bodies (especially unions) and their importance have already been discussed under the principle of subsidiarity. The encouragement of intermediary groups is not sufficient. Because rapid technological developments have made the modern situation so complicated, these intermediary groups are limited in their power and capacity. The result is an impeding and progressive restriction of the initiative and freedom of individuals which comes in the wake of technological change. The wealth of power necessary to cope with this problem of regulation is ultimately lodged in the public authority, whose aim is the common good of all citizens. Of necessity, the powers of government must enlarge to meet the complicated problems of the intensified interaction of groups within society. The public authority, then, should regulate control and orient this complicated process. Governmental regulation may even go as far as nationalization of vital industries if the common good truly demands it. Pius XII explicitly made this point in many of his allocutions and, thus, the added and more complicated role of public authority simply cannot be abandoned nor avoided in the industrialized society of the 1960's.

According to John XXIII, both intermediary groups and government must participate if society is to remain as free as possible for each of its citizens. If the state attempts to regulate everything and thereby destroys free, intermediary bodies, an immoral regime called totalitarianism arises; if the whole sphere of economic and social affairs is abandoned to private groups, the strong crush the weak and society returns to the chaos of a nineteenth-century economic liberalism with all of the attendant abuses of *laissez-faire*. In practice, a correct balance between the two is difficult to achieve and maintain. In underdeveloped countries, for example, the role of the state as economic and social coordinator will be greater because of a lack of formed and responsible intermediary business and union groups. On the other hand, these well-formed intermediary groups in economically advanced countries often pose the problem of monopoly which stifles the initiative and freedom of other citizens.

Thus, the Pope says: "*socialization is one of the characteristic features of our epoch*" (par. 59). It has been brought about by the application of advanced technology to modern society as well as other factors already cited. Historically, the Industrial Revolution has resulted in the urbanization of the world's population. In 1964, for example, eighty percent of the American population lived in metropolitan areas; the tendency is also growing rapidly in Asia and Latin America. This characteristic shift from the farm to the city arises from the demands of an industrialized society, demands which range from the concentration of a labor force to the easy access to transportation for raw materials and finished products. Since this complicated interdependency of peoples affects man's powers to work out his own destiny the natural right of association has become more apparent and necessary. The growth of state power is both an effect and a cause of this natural process, and, as such, the Holy Father recognizes it as an immense good.

> Socialization is, at one and the same time, an effect and a cause of the growing intervention of the state in the areas which, since they touch the deepest concerns of the human person, are not without considerable importance nor devoid of danger. Among these are care of health, instruction and education of the young, control of professional careers, methods of care and rehabilitation of those physically or mentally handicapped in any way. Socialization, however, is also the fruit and expression of a natural tendency almost irrepressible in human beings — the tendency to unite for the purpose of obtaining objectives which each ambitions but which are beyond the capacity of individuals.
>
> This sort of tendency has given rise, especially in these latter decades, to a wide range of groups, associations and institutions having economic, cultural, social, athletic, recreational, professional and political ends. They operate within a single nation and on a world-wide basis (par. 60).

HEALTH, EDUCATION, AND WELFARE

The good which comes from socialization is manifested concretely in the extension and development of man's natural rights in health, education, and welfare (cf. *Pacem in Terris*, pars.

11–13, 18–22). Grants by the state, scholarships of all kinds, public education, and other educational endeavors help promote the natural right of man to develop his talents. Group insurance, social security, compensation, health insurance, and minimal professional competency have given modern man a sense of security never before enjoyed on the earth. These benefits and others are the result of socialization, which is occurring nationally and internationally.

> [Socialization] makes possible, in fact, the satisfaction of many personal rights, especially those of a socio-economic nature. The right to the indispensable means of human subsistence, to health services, to instruction at a higher level, to more thorough professional formation, to housing, to employment, to suitable leisure and to decent recreation are typical examples. In addition, through increasing systematization of modern media of mass communications — press, motion pictures, radio, television — it becomes possible for individuals to participate, as it were, in human events even on a worldwide scale (par. 61).

It is now a commonplace to say that the world has become smaller in size, in communications, in trade, and thus it has become interdependent; this growing socialization of society must now indeed be termed international.

DANGER OF DEPERSONALIZATION

Pope John does not deny that there are distinct disadvantages to the process of socialization. The individual's freedom of initiative is restricted, and the government interferes in many intimate aspects of a man's life.

> At the same time, however, socialization multiplies institutional structures and extends more and more to minute details and juridical control of human relations in every walk of life. As a consequence, it restricts the range of an individual's freedom of action. It uses means, follows methods and creates an atmosphere which make it difficult for one to reach judgments free from eternal pressures, to work on his own initiative, to exercise responsibility and to assert his personality (par. 62).

The great danger here is depersonalization, the supreme bane of human society. Workers in industry become cogs, welfare recipients become cases, neighbors in housing projects become absolute strangers, social security becomes a number, the government becomes a great bureaucracy which controls and regulates by unfeeling laws, liberty of initiative and independence of action become stifled and each person's responsibility becomes limited. In the United States, certain elements in the population, calling themselves conservative, have sensed these disadvantages and, in reaction to them, have branded any governmental interference a reduction of freedom. Undoubtedly, the above disadvantages are real and must be carefully considered in building and planning the social order. Unlike the so-called conservatives, the Holy Father is fundamentally optimistic about the modern world. He knows that socialization and stronger governmental powers do not necessarily mean a diminution of freedom and responsibility, because the advantages of socialization can offset its disadvantages.

> Accordingly, advances in social organization can and should be so brought about that the maximum advantages accrue to citizens while at the same time disadvantages are averted or at least minimized (par. 64).

Since man is a free being, that which he has brought about in freedom can be controlled, and so any disadvantage which arises in the social system can be held to a minimum. In a very real sense, man has in fact been freed from the slavery of fate by socialization. Health insurance and such programs as Medicare have freed men from the instabilities of health; Social Security, from the economic infirmities of old age; automation, from the slavery of back-breaking toil; communications, from the restrictions of time and space. In short, man is "*not forced to become an automaton*": just as socialization was and is the product of man's free will and initiative, by that same free will he can control and humanize the disadvantages of socialization.

SOCIALISM

The question of "*Socialism*" is also treated by Pope John, who explains what he and Pius XI meant by it:

From their basic outline it follows that, in as much as the order of social life is confined to time, it is directed solely to temporal welfare; that since the social relationships of man pertain merely to the production of goods, human liberty is excessively resisted and the true concept of social authority is overlooked (par. 34).

The text is self-explanatory by the three conditions of Socialism mentioned by the Pope: the social order is exclusively temporal, its total object is nothing more than man's temporal good, and finally, the abandonment of any sound notion of social authority. Obviously, no Catholic (or no Christian for that matter) could consent to such a view of the social order. It must be added, however, that *any* social order — capitalism included (or neo-capitalism) — which fulfills this definition would come under the ban of proscription no matter what its name. The important thing to remember is that realities be identified, not simply names (*Pacem in Terris*, par. 159).

It is here that we encounter grave difficulties. The right wing press has made of the word "*socialism*" (as of the word "*liberalism*") a dirty word almost synonymous with communism itself. What definition can we give socialism? State ownership of large capital investments or the means of production? The popes have justified the nationalization of major industries by government when this is truly required by the common good. Group national insurance against old age, unemployment, security, medical needs? The Popes have advocated these measures time and time again as parcel of the common good in our day. Man has the right to these and government is to aid him to secure these rights.

Every man has the right to life, to bodily integrity, and to the means which are necessary and suitable for the proper development of life; these are primarily food, clothing, shelter, rest, medical care and finally the necessary social services. Therefore, a human being also has the right to security in case of sickness, inability to work, widowhood, old age, unemployment, or in any other case in which he is deprived of the means of subsistence through no fault of his own (*Pacem in Terris*, par. 11; cf. par. 64 for the government's role).

If this is what is meant by "*socialism*," then the popes are the greatest socialists who ever lived (inclusive of Karl Marx whose vision hardly surpassed that of the popes in this respect).

HISTORICAL EVOLUTION IN PAPAL TEACHING

In this respect we witness a historical evolution in the texts of the Popes themselves. *Rerum Novarum* of Leo XIII was a coherent attempt to oppose socialism (radical and moderate as a doctrinal whole). His perspective was frankly that the capitalist system of the nineteenth century was basically just and that the wage system was in conformity with the canons of social justice. He attempted to reform the capitalist system by keeping it within the bounds of "*just*" profits and "*just*" wages. Pius XI was even more discriminate in his analysis of Socialism which had evolved tremendously since the days of Leo. He distinguished between the "*revolutionaries*" and the "*reformists,*" and this distinction permitted the Pope to recognize and accept the legitimate grounds on which the total Marxist indictment of the injustices of Capitalism was based. The Pope still rejected this "*moderate socialism*" because even though it has evolved from dogmatic Marxist class warfare, denial of all private property, etc., it was still so opposed to Christian faith that it, too, had to be rejected (*Quadragesimo Anno,* par. 119). This, too, would evolve to the point where 30 years later in *Mater et Magistra* and *Pacem in Terris,* John XXIII frankly incorporates this moderate socialism in fact, if not in name, into his teaching. Nor must the teaching of *Divini Redemptoris* be placed in opposition to this view. The reproaches here of Pius XI against Marxism are directed much more at philosophical and historical materialism than at the criticism Marxism made of the capitalist system (it must also be noted here that the Pope does not exclude another interpretation of Marxism as a social system which would exclude the principles of dialetical and historical materialism. It is on this basis that dialogue with Communists can hope to proceed).

Indications of the Pope's own thought on moderate socialism making its peace with Christianity are clear when he says that it

> seems as if it were drifting toward the truth which Christian tradition has always held in respect, for it cannot be denied that its programs often strikingly approach the just demands of Christian social reformers (*Q.A.*, par. 122).

With *Mater et Magistra* and *Pacem in Terris*, it seems to me, moderate socialism has reached a true peace with Christianity and its reality permeates both encyclicals. *Mater et Magistra* is much more an attack on capitalism than a critique of traditional socialism. Thus socialization is a good and at the service of man (par. 59–62), inequalities must be eliminated (par. 71), a correspondence must be maintained between economic and social progress (par. 73), workers must share in the profits of the industry that accrue from capital investment (par. 75–77), workers should take part in economic decisions at the highest levels (par. 97–100), large corporations and monopolies are criticized (par. 104) — all this is in the tradition of socialist seeking after justice. *Pacem in Terris* goes even further in this respect where peaceful coexistence is assumed and where the struggle is against the conformity and facelessness of neo-capitalist society — a socialism which is no longer tainted with philosophical errors and ideological origins of Marxism, where the economic, social and political aspects of socialism must be considered independently of its theoretical motivations. This is the meaning of the famous par. 159 of *Pacem in Terris*. Paul VI, in a little published (in the U. S.) talk to Italian businessmen, gave one of the most powerful indictments of capitalism I have ever seen. In this respect, he is in the tradition of John XXIII:

> The business enterprise, which by its nature demands collaboration, concord, harmony, is it now still today a clash of minds and of interests? And sometimes, is it not considered an indictment of the one who puts it together, directs it and administers it? Is it not said of you that you are the capitalists and the only guilty ones? Are you not often the target of social dialect? There must be something profoundly mistaken, something radically lacking in the system itself, if it gives rise to such social reactions. It is true that whoever speaks of capitalism today, as many do, with the concepts that defined it in the past century, gives proof of being out of touch with reality. But

> it remains a fact that the socio-economic system generated from Manchesterian Liberalism still persists. It persists in the connection of the one-sidedness of possession of the means of production and of the economy directed toward private profit . . . Such an outlook (materialism) is attributable not only to those who make the fundamental dogma of their unhappy sociology out of an antique dialectic materialism (Communism), but also to the many who erect a golden calf in the place belonging to the God of Heaven and Earth" (*Catholic Messenger*, June 18, 1964, p. 9, or *Social Digest*, October 1964, p. 127).

For the Pope, the capitalistic West is as materialistic as the communist East and being so, it represents a serious temptation to the Church, since the West tries to cloak its political ambitions and basic materialistic intentions in moral terms.

Be that as it may, what is evident from Leo XIII to Paul VI is an evolution of the attitude of the Church toward (moderate) Socialism. Starting with a program to reform capitalism (Leo XIII), there followed a positive program for replacing capitalism (Pius XI, XII), to *de facto* acceptance by the Church of the non-ideological, non-philosophical basis of moderate socialism (John XXIII, Paul VI) as a critique and *point de répère* against neo-capitalism.

NEO-CAPITALISM

Yet, even if this system has not been necessary for the building up of society, it has *de facto* been one of the builders of modern industry in the West, of modern work (with the severe critique we shall give shortly) and of economic advancement in general. It has extended man's mastery over matter and has organized the temporal society of modern times, which, as we have seen, has had and continues to have both its good and bad aspects. It has truly changed the face of the earth in such a way that man is no longer dependent on the elements of nature for his sustenance; he can control nature for his good to the point where famine, drought and overpopulation are becoming less and less a danger. The technology this system has developed is truly astounding in transportation and communication, making the world not only smaller but also widening man's perspective beyond this world to space and beyond. These are the undeniable good consequences of the capitalist system in the West. Yet, we must also recognize just as forcefully the terrible abuse of man which has flowed from this system as well. This new economic-social dynamism has come to disrupt the civilization into which it has been injected, by creating new values and consciences in conformity with the new technological-industrial era in which we live. The nineteenth-century dislocation of man within society is a terrible fact, and our present civilization in the West was built on the broken bones of the millions of overworked and abused proletariat of that country. To a great degree, the modernization we have today has been built on the inhumanities dealt to this class for over a hundred years, much as the Russian revolution produced its economic breakthrough in the twentieth century. The only difference from a moral point of view is that the Russian brutality was shorter than the Western variety. In the economically underdeveloped world, the situation is very serious today. This becomes evident in the case of China. Once humiliated by Western imperialism, she seeks now to displace this influence with her own hegemony in Southeast Asia. In the African states, we have more of an emphasis on modernization for the purpose of self-identification and national unity. This is so because of the artificial boundaries set up by Western colonialism in Africa, as well as the cultural chaos which has resulted from detribalization of the Africans, brought about by the introduction of different religious, cultural, political, and social norms by Western modernizing powers (Christianity, political democracy, industrialism, modern medicine, etc). These all have had a disturbing effect on the traditional tribal unity and form of life of the Africans almost without exception. This, of course, is not to bring a value judgment on these aspects of cultural forms as opposed to those introduced by the West, it is simply to note a fact which becomes more evident every day as violence and disruption increase in the African states.

Yet this subject of social dislocation caused by modern industrialization goes beyond our immediate objective. We shall only note here that any economy — capitalism, socialism, and communism — shall have to determine for each respective system its effects upon the human condition and dignity of man, the power it exercises over their lives as well as its equitable distribution of the produce of labor, before the Christian can give either approval or cooperation with such a regime of production. Thus we come to giving a value judgment on the economic system *because* of its effects on man, while not denying the fact that capitalism has created and transformed a world which has a value in itself (v.g., a theology of terrestrial realities and interpretations of the process of secularization, which does not directly concern us here).

PROFIT SEPARATED FROM WORK

It is here that we meet the very *crux* of our problem with relation to the profit motive of capitalism of the past century, as well as its essentially similar grandchild, neo-capitalism as it exists today in the United States. Profit here is dislocated and has perverted these modern enterprises in a way clearly seen by Marx (and, of course, many before and after him). It is one thing to speak abstractly of profit-capitalism in one's theological chair, and there to work out all sorts of ways which would bring it in conformity with human dignity; it is quite another to examine the historical and factual brutalizing effects, say, on the nineteenth-century proletariat, dominated as it was by economic *laissez-faire* capitalism which, to a very great degree, still infects neo-capitalism in the West, since it suffers from the same congenital disease as its immediate predecessor: profit separated from work, or rather work used as a commodity, sold at a price, in order to make profit for the owners of capital-productive goods along with their stockholders. In such a system, profit takes over as the essential determinant in the whole process of production, with the human factor — work — being nothing more than a means to an end, something to be paid for in the process of making a profit. This was the essential vice of the capitalist system of the nineteenth century, as well as that of the present day, in spite of the fact that its successor's major abuses have been curtailed by welfare legislation to insure some sort of more human distribution of benefits. Thus we have a system in Western societies in which the capitalists have made no real human contribution to the productive process and where the workers are effectively cut off from the fruits of their human labor by "wage" or "salary." Thus the very process of human production is depersonalized and hence, dehumanized. This is exactly what Pius XI said some 30 years ago with regard to the profit-capitalist system. Both labor and capital produce goods, but, in this system, only the capitalists retain profit, while labor simply is given "pay."

> For what else is work but the use or exercise of the powers of mind and body on or by means of these gifts of nature? Now, the natural law, or rather, God's will manifested by it, demands that right order be observed in the application of natural resources to human needs; and this order consists in everything having its proper owner. Hence it follows that unless a man applies his labor to his own property, an alliance must be formed between his toil and his neighbor's property; for each is helpless without the other. This is what Leo XIII had in mind when he wrote: "Capital cannot do without labor, nor labor without capital." It is therefore entirely false to ascribe the results of their combined efforts to either capital or labor alone; and it is flagrantly unjust that either should deny the efficacy of the other, and claim all the product.
>
> Capital, however, was long able to appropriate too much to itself; it claimed all the products and profits, and left to the worker the barest minimum necessary to repair his strength and to ensure the continuance of his class. For by an inexorable economic law, it was held, all accumulation of capital falls to the wealthy, while by the same law the workers are doomed to perpetual want or to a very low standard of life. It is indeed true that the course of things did not always and everywhere correspond with this thesis of the so-called Manchester school; but it cannot be denied that the steady pressure of economic and social tendencies was in this direction. That these erroneous opinions and deceitful axioms should have been vehemently assailed, and not merely by those whom they deprived of their innate right to better their condition,

will assuredly surprise no one (*Quadragesimo Anno*, pars. 53–54).

The evident direction of the Pope's reasoning is that the humanization of production demands the participation of all actors, as well as the equal distribution of profit not just to stockholders and owners of capital goods, but to workers, directors, creditors, etc., according to the quantity and quality of their contribution. For owners to say arbitrarily: "*Here is a price for labor, here is profit*" is a direct dehumanization of the labor process and contrary to the natural law of production. In a primitive economy — without going into the abuses of paternalism — there is no such break, for we have work on a person-to-person basis (craft guilds, even if the major craftsman owned the goods of production); but as the economy becomes more complicated (industrial revolution and its aftermath), it also becomes much more concentrated and the original and personal division of labor no longer figures in production, except as a simple material result ("*work*"), a commodity, a price of merchandise to be used for the purpose of profit production, where profit becomes the end for which all else exists, inclusive of the dignity of human labor. No one shares in the work itself, no one really is interested in the work itself, except as a commodity in the process of production to be deducted from final "*profit.*" It becomes the sole property of the capitalist or stockholder, since in such a system work is nothing else than totally recompensed. Therefore, profit becomes the reward of capital itself, independent of all other factors in production of goods. In classical terms we have here the very definition of capitalism as a profit-motive system, vitiating the system itself and morally repugnant to the Christian as well: an economic system in which capital and work are separated, where the law of contract of wages ("*the iron law of wages*") is the sole meeting between them, and where profit and salary are not only separated, but the latter is actually at the service of the former. Such a system cannot be acceptable to the Christian precisely because of its dehumanizing effects on man's work — his extension in space and time — and such a system has been in fact rejected by John XXIII in *Mater et Magistra.*

MONEY EXISTS FOR MAN, NOT MAN FOR MONEY

Thus it is money and gain which dominates to a very large degree the Western Capitalist system, which has broken and dehumanized generation after generation (in this respect, one has only to read a cursory history of the nineteenth-century labor movement and its conditions). This appetite for gain — the biblical *cupiditas* — was always in men as individuals, for there is no reason to suspect that it is any greater today in men than it was in times past; but what modern capitalism has done is to systematize this vice in the framework of its very economic system *qua system*, and it has become its very reason for being and the law of its institutions, where individuals — inclusive of the individual capitalists themselves — are caught up without remission in this anonymous and dehumanizing violence. The evil is now institutional where its law is profit, and profit alone, and where only institutional and structural reform can make of neo-capitalism a truly humanized and humanizing system. The system carries within itself a type of vicious circle from which, as it now stands, it cannot escape on its own. Capital produces profit, and profit, in its own turn, produces more capital. Christians — from the earliest times — have always condemned this mode of operation among men, even in the (today) often ridiculed aspect of the middle ages where usury was considered an evil. These medieval schoolmen were correct and modern theologians quite wrong, since the former saw very clearly what many religious defenders of Western capitalism have not seen; namely, that any system of economics which dehumanizes man and his labor, where work (taken here in its broadest meaning) and profit are separated, where man's work as an expression and incarnational extension of himself is treated as a commodity used toward a further end — profit — such a system, these ancients saw clearly, was basically inhuman and un-Christian. Money for money's sake, profit for profit's sake, is an aberration from Christianity. Money is for man, not man for money, and it is precisely this vice which infects modern capitalism to its very core, no matter how many laws are passed to curb its abuses. These latter are only palliatives covering its terminal human cancer.

Today this fundamental abuse is contained in the exclusive attribution to the owner of capital goods the surplus benefit of production and to him alone. It is not that he (or they) always keep it for personal fortune but rather that in and of itself, the continuous and progressive investment of these riches into new establishments of production from which the human concept of work is rejected, ends by an automatic multiplication of power which cannot be stopped by itself: technology, unavoidably concentrated economic credit, etc. (which are neither good nor bad in themselves but rather simply technical procedures) have now become the instruments of this appropriation of great riches with its above-mentioned vice. This process, then, is truly "*unnatural*" in its most basic meaning, that is, a dehumanization of man as well as of his extension in space and time: his work.

MAN CANNOT BE BOUGHT

By nature itself, as Pius XI himself said in the passage quoted above, the riches produced belong by right and by nature to him or to those who participated in the production, the fruit of labor belonging to those who actually labored upon it, directly or indirectly, some more quantitatively, others more qualitatively. Certainly, we must admit that a share belongs to the owner of the capital goods themselves, even in a special way, since it is his own labor which has made these good available for others to work upon. But when the work is that of a community — as is the case with every modern enterprise — produced in consort with proprietor, director, and worker, the fruit of that labor belongs to all three categories of man as a community and one cannot morally say (as does the capitalist system today) that one "*pays*" the worker for his work and call it just, with all the remaining profits accruing to the proprietor and stockholder of capital goods. The reason for this is really quite simple. It flows from the fact that neither a man nor his work is a thing one can pay for and leave aside like other types of property in nature; it is generically different from all other types of property. A man cannot be "*bought*" with money or anything else precisely because he and his work are of infinite value. We therefore do great violence to man by separating him from his work by payment only of a salary or wage. By this act, one has robbed him of his most precious possession: his human dignity. This is precisely what profit motive neo-capitalism does today — a vice condemnable philosophically as well as theologically, wherein benefits are distributed as if an enterprise were like other types of property (i.e., to be used for further ends, namely, profit) and not as human dignity demands, a community of labor.

PARTICIPATION OF WORKERS IN SOCIAL EFFORTS

Pope John XXIII, in *Mater et Magistra*, was very cognizant of precisely this problem and suggested various ways in which this inhuman situation of the worker could be ameliorated. Labor, he insisted, must concern itself not only with its private interests, but also with interests which affect the whole social body.

> If we turn our attention to the social field, we see the following developments: the formation of systems of social insurance and, in some more economically advanced states, the introduction of comprehensive social security systems; in labor unions the formation of, and increasing stress on, an attitude of responsibility toward major socio-economic problems; progressive improvement of basic education; an ever wider distribution of welfare benefits; increased social mobility with a consequent lessening of class distinctions; a greater interest in world events on the part of those with an average education (par. 48).

> Modern times have seen a widespread increase in worker associations organized with juridical status in many countries and across national lines. They no longer unite workers for the sake of conflict but rather for joint effort — principally in the field of collective bargaining. But we cannot fail to emphasize how imperative or at least highly opportune it is that the workers should be able freely to make their voices heard, and listened to, beyond the confines of their individual productive units and at every level of society (par. 97).

John approved such participation, and in expanding his suggestions in paragraphs 97–103, he presented the most dynamic as well as the most daring part of the encyclical. His suggestions pass beyond "bread and butter" issues, and strike at the very heart of industrial organization. In the words of Pope John, the workers must proceed from a work contract ("bread and butter" issues such as just wages, vacations, health conditions, insurance, and so on) to a contract of open participation. In paragraph 32, he explained that Leo XIII believed in such power for the worker, and he assumed this power in the present encyclical. For Pope John, worker participation should ultimately end in a contract of partnership through such instruments as cooperatives, profit-sharing, shares and stocks in the company. In *Quadragesimo Anno*, Pope Pius XI had previously mentioned similar cooperation in industrial organization, and here Pope John gave the concept added emphasis. Following the established principle of Pius XII, Pope John did not claim that this kind of participation is a natural right. But he observed that Pius XI had strongly urged such worker participation, and, in paragraph 75 of *Mater et Magistra*, he suggested ways to implement this principle through self-financing by industry and workers, participation by shares, credits, and various other means of active direction and cooperation in the industry itself. Making the thought of Pius XI his own, Pope John insisted that the product of any industry is never the result of one or the other party alone: it is the fruit of both the employer's and the employee's labor. When these aspects of the Pope's theology of work are considered, the concept of *laissez-faire* capitalism is indirectly condemned, as is the theory that only the profit motive regulates industry. Because the workers are co-producers of the product, they are entitled to a greater profit for their labor; it must not all accrue to the owners of industry.

> In this connection, we must recall the principle proposed by
> obtained by the joint effort of the one and the other And it
> our predecessor Pius XI in *Quadragesimo Anno:* "It is totally
> false to ascribe to capital alone or to labor alone that which is

> is flagrantly unjust that either should deny the efficacy of the other and seize all the profits" (par. 76).
>
> Experience suggests that this demand of justice can be met in many ways. One of these, and among the most desirable, is to see to it that the workers, in the manner that seems most suitable, are able to participate in the ownership of the enterprise itself. For today, more than in the times of our predecessor, "every effort . . . must be made that at least in the future a just share only of the fruits of production be permitted to accumulate in the hands of the wealthy, and that a sufficiently ample share be supplied to the workingmen" (par. 77).

This just sharing, John said, "*is a demand of justice*" in our day, and a matter of strict justice, not a concession by the corporation, since it is more than probable that the worker's labor has gone into the wealth allotted to further productivity and expansion. It is another way in which the Pope saw a more widely diffused ownership of private property in modern society. And while suggestions on how this is to be accomplished are contingent, the concept of co-partnership is not, and, because it is not, it "*is a demand of justice.*"

Since there are many ways of actively sharing in industrial and economic profit, John XXIII did not attempt to give specific means of accomplishing this end. The question of profit sharing becomes more complex when it is observed that each industry reinvests a portion of the profits in a renovation of machinery, new construction, expansion of plants, and so on. All this necessary reinvestment is done by the profit which was earned by both industry and labor, and while it is obvious that all of the profit cannot be shared directly, part of the dividends and capital investment can be shared by such means as stocks and bonds. The workers' participation in the actual property of the concern is not merely an act of generosity or efficiency (for instance, a further incentive for more and better production), but desirable in itself as a title of justice (see paragraph 32 for the same idea). In the Pope's mind, the corporation is to become closer to what its name implies: a corporation of both workers and employers who share a mutual responsibility and dignity that proceeds from the ownership of the one and same concern. Corporation in this sense is a true and concrete application of what the Pope means by "*socialization*," one of the main themes of the letter.

PARTICIPATION IN MANAGEMENT

Obviously, the ramifications of corporate participation in industry include a great deal more than a "passive" profit sharing which is becoming more common in America. The worker, insisted the Pope, must be given a true voice — direct or representative — in the actual management of the industry. For a worker to receive more money is not, strictly speaking, more human; to add a greater human dimension to his role in industry, the worker must accept responsibility, and this can come through an active participation in industrial ownership and management. In paragraphs 91 through 93, the Pope underlines this expanding role for the worker:

> Following the line of thought of our predecessors, we defend the desire of employees to participate actively in the management of enterprises in which they are employed. It is not feasible to define a priori the manner and extent of participation of this sort. Such matters must be decided with an eye to specific conditions prevailing in each enterprise. These conditions vary from enterprise to enterprise, and indeed, within the same enterprise frequently undergo sudden and profound changes.
>
> We have no doubt, however, that workers should be allowed to play an active part in the affairs of an enterprise — private or public — in which they are employed. At any rate, every effort should be made that industrial enterprises assume the characteristics of a true human community whose spirit influences the dealings, duties and role of each of its members (par. 91).
>
> This indeed demands that relations between employers and directors on the one hand, and employees on the other, be marked by respect, appreciation, understanding, loyal and active co-operation, and devotion to their common undertaking. It also requires that the work be viewed and carried out by all the members of the enterprise, not merely as a source of

> income, but also as the fulfillment of a duty and the performance of a service to others. As a result, the workers should have a timely say in, and be able to make a welcome contribution to the efficient development of the enterprise.
>
> Our predecessor, Pius XII, remarked that the economic and social function, which every man aspires to fulfill, demands that the activity of each be not completely subjected to the will of others. A humane view of the enterprise ought undoubtedly to safeguard the authority and necessary efficiency associated with unity of direction. It does not follow that those who are daily involved in an enterprise must be reduced to the level of mere silent performers who have no chance to bring their experience into play. They must not be kept entirely passive with regard to the making of decisions that regulate their activity (par. 92).
>
> Finally, attention must be called to the fact that the desire for a greater exercise of serious responsibility on the part of the workers in various productive units corresponds to lawful demands inherent in human nature. It is also in conformity with progressive historical developments in the economic, social and political fields (par. 93).

The reason for this expanded view of the worker's role is that the professional man perfects himself by and through the work he does. In a very special way, his work expresses his personality, and, as such, it ought to be a true expression of himself. This reflection of the worker's personality in his work cannot be achieved except through responsibility, which in turn cannot be realized without an effective voice in the enterprise in which he works. In his work, a man's actions must be those of a free and responsible human being; and for most men, this is almost impossible without an effective sharing in what they do. A man's humanity is expressed in his economic activity, and if this is not free and responsible, his work lacks human dignity. When a man has the opportunity, which is rightfully his, to perfect his human dignity by and through his daily work, his work then represents, in a true sense, a reflection of his person, which is made in the image of God.

This basic insistence on the worker's full sharing in the industrial structure, a tenet that pervades John XXIII's social thought, may seem like a fond dream and not a practical end which is possible to attain. From one viewpoint it is a dream; but to be more accurate, it is an ideal that does not now exist. Yet such an ideal can be brought into existence in a society which is truly personalistic and where all forms of private property are open to the use and possession of all individuals. The Pope's personalistic vision of society lies between the total collectivism and socialistic communism, which merges the individual into a sort of amorphous glob, and the tooth and claw *laissez-faire* capitalism which does not serve the individual from social consideration. In this Christian social order described by Pope John, man becomes more conscious of his freedom and his responsibility, and thus participates more humanly in the economic and political structures to which he belongs.

POLITICAL DEMOCRACY WITHOUT ECONOMIC DEMOCRACY

From this point of view, Americans are at opposite poles in political democracy and economic democracy. In the former, each American participates and contributes according to his talents, abilities, and needs. He takes full responsibility as a citizen because political institutions are ultimately directed by him through his representatives. According to *Pacem in Terris* (par. 26–27), this political participation is a basic demand of human nature, and corresponds to human dignity because it gives each man a sense of duty and responsibility. Economic society has no such democracy, because no responsibility exists for the promotion of human dignity. Insofar as the direction of an enterprise is concerned, the worker is a perpetual minor, a number that can be dismissed or hired according to the "*need*" determined solely by market demand. His muscles and professional skills are needed, but his opinion and consent are never requested. He is an automaton who is turned on or off. And this view of a man violates all canons of social justice given by the Pope, for the precise reason that an automaton cannot be or develop as a human being. In such a view of man, often assumed by Western capitalism, human dignity and human work are a "*commodity to be sold,*" a cynical view condemned over a hundred years ago by Karl Marx. Until this attitude can be corrected by active participation in industry, the worker's human dignity must remain truncated.

The directives in *Mater et Magistra* are meant to remedy this dehumanizing situation. Though the average American factory worker took home a record $125 a week in 1964, his gain in human dignity was not commensurate. To Pope John, an industry or an enterprise is not only a profit-making institution, but also a community of persons (par. 93). His understanding of the responsibility of unions to consider the common good (par. 48) and of the need for both workers and employers to cooperate in their proper enterprise clearly demonstrates his view of industry as a community:

> We believe further that one must praise in the same way the outstanding endeavors performed in a true Christian spirit by our beloved sons in other professional groups and workers' associations which take their inspiration from natural-law principles and show respect for freedom of conscience (par. 102).

This type of spirit corresponds to the human dignity of workers because it encourages the development of their sense of responsibility toward the industry itself. Yet this end is impossible to achieve without an effective copartnership, cooperation, coownership. In Catholic social thought, John XXIII has surpassed all other Popes in his trust and encouragement of the worker in a free society. The ideal social system is not a socialistic, communistic, or capitalistic system; rather, it is that system which best promotes human dignity by increasing opportunities for freedom and responsibility in the work to which both worker and employer contribute.

PERFECTING PERSONALITY BY EXERCISING RESPONSIBILITY

The dignity and personality of the worker are central in paragraphs 82–84 of *Mater et Magistra:*

> Justice is to be observed not only in the distribution of wealth acquired by production, but also with respect to the conditions

> under which production is achieved. For there is an innate demand in human nature that when men engage in production they should have the opportunity of exercising responsibility and of perfecting their personalities (par. 82).
>
> It follows that if the organization and operation of an economic system are such as to compromise the human dignity of those who engage in it, or to blunt their sense of responsibility, or to impede the exercise of personal initiative, such an economic system is unjust. And this is so even if, by hypothesis, the wealth produced through such a system reaches a high level and this wealth is distributed according to standards of justice and equity (par. 83).
>
> It is not possible to describe in detail the sort of economic organization which is more conformed to the dignity of man and more suited to developing his sense of responsibility. Nevertheless, our predecessor Pius XII opportunely sketches the following directive: Small and average-size undertaking in agriculture, in the arts and crafts, in commerce and industry, should be safeguarded and fostered through entry into co-operative unions; in the large concerns, meanwhile, there should be the possibility of modifying the work contract by one of partnership (par. 84).

Obviously, a mere multiplication of economic goods or material benefits does not, of itself, enhance human dignity, so both communism and capitalism fall under the same censure when their goals are solely concerned with the material advancement of man. In a sense, East and West suffer from different forms of the same cancer: materialism. According to the Pope, that system alone is moral which permits man free initiative and responsibility in his work. The American system has elevated man's material stature, as the Communist system may someday do; yet this does not make them moral or human. A man's dignity is not necessarily increased by the number of autos and gadgets he owns, but by the intellectual, psychological, and moral fulfillment of his personality through the work which he does. The worker must never be reduced to a passive agent in the production and consumption of goods. The role of a robot, a cog in a consumptive machine, does not correspond to the dignity of man. For the worker, responsibility for production must be added to the consumption of production if America is to attain a human, economic democracy. And since one of the great threats to American society comes from the destruction of personality by impersonal work, the only way to counteract this uniformity of mass production and mass frustration is for man's participation in society through work to become more human by responsibility. Thus, the *insistence* of John XXIII on copartnership and sharing in enterprise.

II. THE RIGHT USE OF PROPERTY

Thus we must come to the general conclusion at this point that the property of production is property only in an analogous sense, a special type of property to which we simply cannot apply what Marx called the "*iron law of wages,*" nor the "*hidden hand*" of market demand of Adam Smith, nor the law of supply and demand, for the simple reason that capital property is a property incarnate within a human society or community, an enterprise and community, so that if this is destroyed by the all-pervading and all-commanding profit motive, the vicious circle which we discussed above is established and the human person degraded (along with his work) as a means to a further end, namely, profit. Karl Marx with all of his errors in economics and despite his ideological fervor, saw this all very clearly and, at bottom, his was a human and humanistic protestation against such human degradation which establishes the profit motive by means of such a rupture. This is to denature the meaning of both property and work understood in their human and Christian meaning. It is not the fact alone of having capital goods which gives one the right to the exclusive fruit of capital (this is a perversion); it is rather the quantitative and qualitative human collaboration of the proprietor, and this in accordance with the measure of his human engagement within the enterprise itself. If then capitalism as a system is accepted as having as its direct and final object the regime of profit, where, in other words, profit alone regulates the economy and its distribution of wealth among the diverse sectors of the economy, then the only way out for the Christian is to eliminate such a system. Where market values above all else determine the livelihood of millions of men and women, we are surely in the realm of the pure perversion of man by man. Man's livelihood and his dignity come to him to a great degree by and through his work — taken in its broadest meaning — and this aspect of his being cannot be separated from him because, for instance, the capitalist no longer has any need of him since there is no longer any "profit" in conducting a particular business with the painful result that the worker — blue or white collar — is thrown on the slag heap of indigence, welfare, or even starvation. It is a crime against humanity which cries to heaven for vengeance and from whose ultimate logic, at least in the West, we have unfortunately not graduated since the essential evil remains.

RELATIONSHIP BETWEEN LABOR AND PROFIT

It has not been simply the abuses of capitalism as a system which have made of it a vicious system for man (and therefore cannot be corrected by one or a multiplicity of welfare laws, such as anti-trust legislation); its vice proceeds from its very nature as it conceives the relationship between human labor and the profit motive, between capital and work. Its very constitution is vitiated by a disassociation of workers from the enterprise (which, as we have seen, John XXIII clearly saw as a phenomenon which must be overcome), from new enterprises built by the profit of the collaboration of both (which Pius XI clearly saw back in 1931). In the present structure of the capitalist system, all profit, all capital expansion belongs to proprietor and stockholder, and to him alone, to the exclusion of all other collaborators in the enterprise.[1] It thus denies the concept of the enterprise as a collaboration of a human community, it denies the human solidarity of worker and proprietor in the production of goods and finally reduces the worker to nothing more than a mere *"hired hand"*

[1] It is interesting to note the beginnings of a major breakthrough in the demands made by Walter Reuther and the United Auto Workers of America. In substance, their claim was that workers should also be co-owners of the company in the form of profit sharing and other communitarian goals.

to be discarded when he is no longer "*profitable*." It then denies the human community of work which the enterprise is supposed to be. It denies the fact that work in the production of goods is social in nature and is brought about by a collaboration of all. It is not divisible like other property of a purely material nature, *partim et partim*. The very social constitution of an enterprise is that of a community of human collaborators, each sharing in all the fruits of production to the degree of his participation in the work; a consortium, in short, of proprietor, director, stockholder, and worker together producing the riches involved, where each must share in the same riches produced (and re-invested) in a social manner as well. Certainly, investments have a right to a profitable return, but neo-capitalism has inversed the human and social ends of the economy and the enterprise with the result that it no longer has as its direct object and final end the consortium of human collaboration in an enterprise, but rather pure profit; where all other considerations are not only secondary but expendable as well if the enterprise is not "*solvent*" (cf. in the U. S., the outstanding examples of Appalachia, migrant workers, "*wetbacks*"; where it is the government who must shoulder the burden after the capitalist system has shoved thousands of able men on a human slag heap to starve or shift for themselves). This type of inhumanity has been and continues to be endemic to this system itself, not an accidental by-product of it.[2] These are institutional defects not, as the scholastics would say, *accidentaliter* but *substantialiter*. It is simply useless in trying to make the individuals within these institutions "*virtuous*" or "*charitable*" since the defect is not individual but structural.

DO ECONOMIC INSTITUTIONS PROMOTE HUMAN DIGNITY?

The situation cannot be solved by armchair theoreticians or theologians who can take up all kinds of hypotheses *in abstracto*, for men do not live abstractly nor do institutions. Rather, as Christians and as human beings, we must look directly at what

---

[2] A somewhat attenuated same view can be found in J. K. Galbraith, *The New Industrial State* (Boston, 1967) pp. 262–281.

these institutions actually do to men and for what motive they are directed and conducted. For the Christian (and for the true human person) there is really only one criterion for any enterprise within the context of any economy: whether it promotes (or not) the human dignity of the men who collaborate within it. This reference to man as person and as incarnate spirit must remain for the theologian a permanent light and final criterion of each historical evolution of the economy, be it moderate socialism, communism, or capitalism. It is instructive in this respect that this is exactly what has happened in the papal teachings on private property, where the popes have criticized both extremes of denial of private property (communism) as well as that of individualistic capitalism. We have seen that even moderate socialism during the era of Pius XI had made progress along these lines, breaking away from the dogmatic denial of private property by orthodox Marxists. There has, parallel to this evolution, been a similar one in the teachings of the Popes.

III. SOCIAL RESPONSIBILITY OF PRIVATE PROPERTY

In recent years, expanded notions of the concept of private property have developed, and from a dynamically comprehensive point of view, Pope John proceeded to adjust these new developments to the traditional concept of private property. Among these new developments are changes which have occurred in industrial management, in ownership of capital goods, in professional ability and competence, and the creation of various types of sickness and old age insurance which have replaced patrimonies as the source of security for old age and survivors. These and other modern developments have modified the use of private property in the workaday life of many citizens, and in effect, modern society now faces a new situation. But though this new condition of modern society modifies the traditional concept, the right of individual citizens to own and administer private property is not destroyed (*Mater et Magistra*, par. 104–121).

To understand Pope John's reconsideration of the concept of private property, it must be made clear that the right usage is prior to and conditions the right to private property. God has created man as a body and a soul, an incarnate being, and as such, man has a natural right to use the world's goods for the conservation of his life, the fruition of his talents, and the protection of his health. This right precedes the right of property, and in traditional Catholic social thought, the right to property is a derivative, or a concretization, of the right of usage. In other words, the right to use material goods is fundamental and primary, while the right to own material goods is secondary and derived. The right to property exists so that an order might be established by which the right of usage is assured and guaranteed.

The right of property is a means to an end, and it is therefore subordinate to the right of usage, the end itself. Since every means is relative, the doctrine of the *absolute* right of private property is a grave social aberration. Clearly, then, private property must ultimately promote the right of usage. For example, large land holdings in the hands of a few Latin Americans represent a serious disorder because the right of usage is denied to the many. To correct this disorder, agrarian reform is a pressing need of social justice in many of these Latin American countries. Property is thus a social responsibility, and it must be used to promote the general welfare. The social responsibility which accrues to the right of private property is a fundamental concept in the social thought of recent Popes (cf. *Mater et Magistra*, par. 43). This paragraph is a clear development of the idea of Pius XII's radio message of 1941. In this message, Pius XII stated:

> Every man, as a living being gifted with reason, has in fact from nature the fundamental right to make use of the material goods of the earth, while it is left to the will of man . . . to regulate in greater detail the actuation of this right. This individual right cannot in any way be suppressed, even by other clear and undisputed rights over material goods. Undoubtedly, the natural order, deriving from God, demands also private property . . . But all this remains subordinate to the natural scope of material goods and cannot emancipate itself from the first and fundamental right which concedes their use to all men. (On the anniversary of *Rerum Novarum*)

The words of Pius XII are clear and Pope John simply makes

them his own. This concept of the right of usage is further emphasized in *Pacem in Terris:*

> The right to private property, even of production goods, also derives from the nature of man. This right, as we have elsewhere declared, is an effective aid in safeguarding the dignity of the human person and the free exercise of responsibility in all fields of endeavor. Finally, it strengthens the stability and tranquility of family life, thus contributing to the peace and prosperity of the commonwealth (par. 21).
>
> However, it is opportune to point out that there is a social duty essentially inherent in the right of private property. This principle of social philosophy allows for such necessities in modern social life as agrarian reform, the nationalization of basic industries in case of true public need, the right of eminent domain, and civil rights legislation, which demands equal public accommodations for all citizens (par. 22).

All of these considerations on the right of usage do not change or supplant the natural right to own private property, though some persons have made such a conclusion after a rapid reading of the encyclical. A closer examination, however, will show that this interpretation is not correct. On the contrary, the right to private property is more important today than ever before, and though Pope John wants to expand the concept of private property to include recent developments, his argument rests solely on traditional thought. In short, the Pope wants to show that private property is a relative right and not absolute, as the nineteenth-century Manchestarian liberals maintained.

PROFESSIONAL SKILLS

The Pope's argument to expand the concept of private property comes out of his keen understanding of the new conditions in modern economic society. Until comparatively recent times, most people lived on farms. To most farmers, the normal means to security was a patrimony of stable capital goods which could be depended upon to provide food and shelter. Today, a man provides security for himself and his family through such things as health, survivor, and old-age insurance. Above all, however, a man today no longer makes his livelihood by his work on a farm; he does so by virtue of his professional skill. Over seventy percent of the people in modern Western society live in metropolitan areas and derive their livelihood directly from their professional skills. This demand for professional skill is becoming so prevalent that in the next five to ten years students without technical training, or "*dropouts*," will have no possibility of finding work.

This shift from the dependence on capital goods to professional skills is an important effect of socialization (see the Pope's discussion in pars. 59–62), and as such, is to be considered a step forward. By its very nature, socialization has been both the cause and the effect of the complexity and the enrichment of our modern civilization, and since the process of socialization has been intensified through the increasing interrelationships of professional and technical skills, these skills must now be an integral part of any consideration of modern civilization. Through these complex interrelationships, the objective culture of mankind has been enriched; that is, the objective elements such as art, architecture, painting, writing, technology, and so on, which are realized by human labor and which transform the world. In its turn, the objective culture has enriched the subjective culture of humanity: that is, each person in a society perfects himself scientifically, intellectually, culturally, morally, and in every way possible, limited only by his will and abilities. This enrichment has been brought about through the specialization in professional and technical skills by an ever-increasing number of people in modern society. Their dependency is no longer on a patrimony of capital goods, but on these acquired professional abilities. The Pope considers this form of security as a better expression of the human personality, and these abilities and the social security which comes out of them must now rank in equal importance with the traditional patrimony of private property.

IV. STAGES OF DEVELOPMENT

Thus, the capitalist system is not something of a temporal value or permanence and, as we pass into an age of automation, a whole new mental reference must begin to be applied to the economy. In a sense, we have here a hope and an opportunity for the future, a breaking away from the past. We shall deal with this at length in the remainder of this paper.

We see the error of certain moralists who still speak of the "law" of supply and demand, as if we were still in the nineteenth century, and as if, as Pope John remarked, we had made no progress in our knowledge of or control over the economy. The essential problem today for all those concerned with human dignity is how exactly to evolve from the profit-motive, salary-wage system of the past to the type of human enterprise which *Mater et Magistra* says is today not a matter of charity, but rather, under new conditions, a matter of *strict justice*. The problem is to evolve from this present system to that of the consortium and human community of work. To do this, we must study both the causes as well as the consequences of this rupture between human labor and production, if we are to approach the problem from a human and Christian point of view.

HISTORICAL EVOLUTION

Our analysis in the previous pages of profit and of the capitalist system which produces it as its end and law has shown it to be diametrically opposed to the human and Christian spirit. What factors, then, are historically responsible for this present human chaos in the economy, that is, the progressive separation of man from the fruits of his labor, between material goods and the men who produced them? Between property and work, between private benefits and the social function of work and the enterprise between profit and service?

What we can see very clearly is that these two *termini* have been effectively disjointed and separated, with the nefarious result that from human collaboration in the enterprise we have presently come to the aberration of profit seeking as the prime motive for and in itself. Thus the whole orientation of the system itself has become corrupt at its very core. In this historical evolution, we can, I believe, distinguish three distinct stages: (1) personal capitalism, (2) the capitalistic system, and finally (3) speculative capitalism. The nomenclature is really unimportant but what these terms signify is, as I shall argue, quite correct. By this progressive linear development we proceed to an increasing dehumanizing of the human person by the omnipotent direction and law of profit. Thus the economy becomes, in a strict sense, an inhuman economy. Let us rapidly trace this evolution.

PERSONAL CAPITALISM

We have here a great deal of bold initiative. Work, besides being the part and parcel of this enthusiast, is done in direct or indirect collaboration with others in a true enterprise. Man is a real creator here by taming and organizing the world of nature by his rationalization of the brutal milieu. He opens the way for others and prepares the terrain for others who would come to further develop what he has initiated. Money and capital are, however, instrumental for this purpose and spontaneously laid to the action of its proprietor. It can be the work either of an individual or of a group, but the rights here to the fruits of the enterprise are founded on effective responsibilities, personal and in collaboration. What is foremost in intent is the service rendered to men and not the profit to be derived from it. The old forms of paternalism were strides in the history of the economy but, in a sense, it was much more human than the large anonymous corporation of today. In paternalism, at least the capital rested in an instrumental function of its place within the society of persons, where both proprietor and worker were united — even if only indirectly — in a true human enterprise, a *consortium* of labor and work, of profit and work, of worker and proprietor.

THE CAPITALIST SYSTEM

The capitalist system is the second stage of development of modern economy where we "progress" from personal labor and consortium to the anonymous system of stockholder-director, where profit and labor are effectively disjoined. Here we have the first true rupture in modern times between human elements which are humanly co-essential in the enterprise of work. Here for the first time, modern man becomes alienated from the product of his hands and the essential vice of the capitalist system appears in all of its stark inhumanity. Capital, direction and work are effectively separated and each becomes alienated from the other. (It is here that, with some truth, Marx places the origins of class hatred and struggle in the poorer economies.) Capital is owned by the anonymous corporation of stockholders who do not work, have no (practical) say in the direction (run by a board of directors), and simply exist to gain profit, and the investment is solely for profit. The workers are separated from their work by a "*wage*" or "*salary*" and the inhuman system is thus created: capitalism. There is no interest in human work, no social responsibility ("*limited liability*") for the enterprise itself, just as long as it returns a "*profit.*" In colloquial English, they wouldn't give a damn about human factors of production. The enterprise is in the hands of a few men who assure the stockholders of a good return on their investment. Profit here is no longer the result of personal engagement and responsibility of proprietor, director, and worker, but becomes the aim of the whole enterprise so as to give a good return to the anonymous stockholders who have no interest, no personal engagement in the enterprise.

SPECULATIVE CAPITALISM

Speculative capitalism is the final evolution of the process. With this system, we reach thc nadir of inhumanity of the whole capitalistic system. Federalization of vast powers is in the hands of a few men. This can be clearly seen from a simple example. The one hundred largest manufacturing corporations in the U. S. in 1962 controlled fifty-eight percent of the net capital assets (financial, land, buildings, and equipment) of all manufacturing corporations. Virtually no attention is given to this vast accumulation of power and economic concentration, except in a small study made by Democratic Senator Hart of Michigan. Economist

Gardiner C. Means testifies that business concentration is vast and growing; it is worse than it was in 1929, in spite of all the antitrust suits. Economic director Willard Mueller of the Federal Trade Commission tells of a new gimmick now thriving amazingly — absorption by merger — which seems to be out of reach of the old-fashioned Sherman Act (1890) and Clayton Act (1914).

Gardiner Means gives some impressive figures. He recalls that the nation was shocked in 1929 at business concentration; it amounted perhaps to forty-four percent of the total "*net capital assets*" of "*all manufacturing corporations.*"

Now the figure has gone up to fifty-eight percent, and is still growing. He says: "*There has been a very considerable increase in concentration in manufacturing as a whole in the last 33 years.*" The result has been that the flexibility of price compensation is reduced; we have administered prices and wages, and the small units have to go along. Let factories and men be idle, administered prices do not fall; prices actually rose in some of President Eisenhower's recessions.

Mr. Means lists the one hundred manufacturing giants that have a mortgage on the rest of the country, but here we will give only the top ten, the pride of the nation, with total assets:

1. Standard Oil (N. J.) — $10.4 billion
2. General Motors — $10.2 billion
3. Ford — $5.4 billion
4. U. S. Steel — $5 billion
5. Gulf Oil — $4.2 billion
6. Texaco — $4.16 billion
7. Socony Mobil Oil — $4.13 billion
8. Standard Oil (Calif.) — $3.4 billion
9. Standard Oil (Ind.) — $3.1 billion
10. E. I. Dupont — $3 billion

(If you want to know "Number 100" on the list, it is Armour and Company, the meat packers, with $436,100,000 in total assets.)

America in terms of the cliché favors checks and balances in its political structure, and used to feel that economic power ought also somehow to be diffused rather than concentrated. That was the notion behind the Sherman and Clayton Acts, and of Teddy Roosevelt. But that has now been changed. The quiet revelations before Senator Hart's subcommittee got almost no attention at all.

Economist Corwin Edwards and others testified that antitrust laws are pretty much out of date. They were designed to keep a 1910 Goliath, Inc. from gobbling up a small competitor. Today, the capitalist system merges not just potential competitors, but subsidiaries in alien fields, producing what witnesses called the "*conglomerate enterprise.*" GM doesn't just manufacture Chevrolets, it makes refrigerators and diesel locomotives. The Columbia Broadcasting Corporation buys the New York Yankees. Martin-Marietta makes concrete pipe and sophisticated space-craft equipment. Dr. Walter Adams, of Michigan State University, points out that Olin Mathieson can give you farm chemicals, sporting goods, or a very fine brand of toothpaste; General Dynamics runs from sand and gravel to Atlas missiles. Textron is an amalgam of 27 separate divisions and 113 separate plants: it has a line of helicopters, chicken feed, chain saws, and work shoes, along with lawn mowers and bathroom accessories.

These are not monopolies (in the traditional sense) they are "*conglomerates,*" and conglomerate giantism is growing. Dr. Adams thinks it's "*the least conscionable form of economic powers. The Public Utility Act (1935) split electric holding companies from functionally unrelated operations, but what was banned for them has broken out all over the lot in other industries.*"

"*I am against private Socialism of concentrated private power as thoroughly as I am against government Socialism,*" FDR said in 1935.

How do these immensities work? Staff Researcher John Blair finds that once immense is always immense; a giant conglomerate can pour its power into secondary lines and absorb competitors. There was "*the Great Merger Movement*" around 1900, but another one is going on now, says Dr. Mueller. Between 1951–1963, the 200 biggest immensities made 1,956 acquisitions. They didn't absorb sick companies, but profitable ones.

GIANTS WITH VAST POWER

We have taken the trouble to show what has happened to speculative capitalism in one Western nation. These giants are not interested in the actual production of goods, but pure speculation based on the profit motive, not to satisfy a social need by an economic good, but thinking only of themselves in a regime of pure profit. This is the age of Wall Street speculators, of share trading, of the up and down points of Dow-Jones averages, panic buying and selling — totally inhuman activity separated from all care of consortium or human product of labor, whose sole function is to make money; entrepreneurs and speculators who are really parasites on the work of other men, where we have an absolute disassociation of direction, capital and workers of any one or many enterprises. We have here the vast trusts and monopolies of vast power for evil on an international scale which, since their sole object is pure profit, couldn't care less for the human problems which are posed in each country, each particular sector where one or another enterprise is located. Money in this system no longer goes to workers nor to stockholders, but is continuously redirected within a closed circle of capital ruled only by its own law of profit. All ties with man are broken and thereby capitalism has attained its proper end and moral corruption. When a crop will not bring in correct profits, it is burned, as was done recently in Columbia with its coffee, leaving thousands to beg or starve, all because the Columbian-American coffee interests and trusts so dictated it. One telephone call from United Fruit headquarters in New York to practically any country in Latin America means profit or indigence for many within that country. The extent of its economic powers on an international scale are simply unknown, but one thing we do know: its own interest becomes its own end before which everything must give way, including the national or even international common good. Such power can destroy a whole political order (as has happened many times in Latin America), engenders insecurity for prices and markets, reduces millions of men to a whim and wish of a tiny few, while all the time preparing a materialistic culture of profit and gain as the first and only law of life.[3] Such a structure is not offended by war itself, since it shares in the great profits made from government contracts in its huge war machine (Vietnam). Antitrust laws are palliatives to curb such a system's more blatant abuses, but the source of its abberation remains within it. Even in the area of palliatives, how very difficult is it to get these enterprises to do something to correct the terrible injustices they inflict on an unsuspecting public such as water, air and cultural pollution! What can be done to once again progressively humanize this system?

FINAL OBSERVATIONS

We have already pointed out one such attempt, and that by John XXIII in a section of *Mater et Magistra* which we have already seen. Furthermore, from a Christian and human point of view, man in the economic sphere (as in all other spheres as well, one might add) must be made once again the master and the end of production. This was the objective of John XXIII as well as our own. As a theologian, my objective here is not to give technical solutions to this vast problem, but it is the duty of the theologian to keep before man's eyes the fact that man must be the end and the means of any economic system. This implies a return from the traditional Capitalist system insofar as this system alienates man in the above-mentioned sense. Man is the end and master of property in general and of productive goods in particular. This was what John XXIII meant when he spoke about social responsibility of workers *within* the enterprise. Such a task can only be performed by once again connecting his personality with the product of the enterprise. This is the first relationship between man and material goods, namely, that it is his incarna-

[3] In this respect, see the encyclical of Pope Paul VI, *Populorum Progressio*, par. 61–65.

tion and extension in space and time, and as such co-essential to his person, and therefore participant in his personal dignity. To use man for profit is more than materialism, it is a desecration of this incarnate spirtually material being who is man, coexistentially. The evolution of capitalism is one direction which man's relationship with matter has taken and this has ended in human failure. As Christians we cannot and must not see anything eternal or fatalistic about it, flowing as it were "*from the laws of nature*." This was the profound error of the physiocrats of the eighteenth century and continues today in those who think that the system in its basic tenets cannot be changed. In fact, with modern socialization it not only can but must change to meet the absolute need of human society for responsibility. In our efforts at transformation, we must aim at transforming the system itself from that of pure profit to a system of work for man. This will, ultimately, entail a new entity different from neo-capitalism. We must occupy the middle ground between the two extremes of absolute state collectivism (communism) and the regime of profit-end (neo-capitalism). The Popes have situated this humanizing economy and social vision between the two, taking what was most human in both systems in what we call "*moderate Socialism*" where property, capital, and government regulations are guided by one principle and one principle only: the promotion of the dignity of man, and where everything else, in the final Christian analysis, is a means to this end. This is the view of the Popes who contemplate no ideology, no crusade, no "sacred" property rights, no dogmatic state intervention — none of these can be an absolute. They are all relative to human dignity and must be used or not used according as they promote this dignity. We must not say that we keep an economic institution while keeping the dignity of man (this is a perversion of priorities), but we must say that we keep an institution in order to safeguard and promote human dignity, for we know only too well to what dehumanization of the economy, what depersonalization this profit-motive capitalism has led us for well over a century. It needs reform from its core outwards.

COLLECTIVE EFFORTS AND REWARDS

We must, with John XXIII, attempt to find and define within the enterprise, those things which cannot be separated and their mutual interdependence if we are to have a human system of production: property, instruments of production, direction, work, credit, and profit. All rights to the fruits of this common production are founded only on a human presence which, in its turn, gives an enterprise its human and communitarian aspect which is responsible for production and distribution of its fruits. This is so — as we have said — because the property of an enterprise is not property like other property, since it produces goods and services in conjunction with and not separated from the infinite dignity of the work of human beings who therefore have a right to share in its effective distribution, profit, and re-investment. It is a type of collective effort and rewards, whose appropriations are not given to an exclusive group but rather determined by a type of qualitative distribution of profit. Of its very nature, this distribution confers on each of the participants in the communitarian enterprise rights which are differential and specific; that of the owner of capital actually engaged in the enterprise over which he has direct responsibility; that of workers whose rewards must respect the qualitative and quantitative variants of each individual's participation in the work of the enterprise; that of the stockholder whose position, humanly speaking, is much more precarious than that of the former two, for capital as such has no rights for it does no work. Yet, it is just that the investor receives some return since it is only thanks to his investment that proprietor and worker can produce, sharing together what is the responsibility of all. Thus, this is much more than a simple mathematical distribution of profit, for in the final analysis it is the communitarian aspect of an enterprise — stockholder, properietor, director, worker — which establishes and guarantees the rights of persons to the fruit of that enterprise. By it, and by it alone, do we have a true integration of persons within the enterprise itself, where none are alienated, neither from the enterprise, nor from its work, nor from its profit. Only in such a system will the dualism of "*salary payment — capital profit*" be effectively healed and integrated within a complete whole. With this synthetic principle, the inhumanity of Capitalism is overcome, a system which has economically and spiritually separated and, by separating, ruined these two inseparable poles of human life. The dialectic between the two must once again be established.

CHAPTER III

CHRISTIANITY AND ATHEISM: A DIALOGUE?

In his first encyclical, *Ecclesiam Suam*, Pope Paul VI wrote that atheism "is the most serious problem of our time" (par. 104). The reason is twofold, namely, that such ideological systems . . . deny God and oppress the Church — by systems that are often identified with economic, social and political regimes, among which atheistic communism is the chief (par. 105). The dialogue in such circumstances is, admittedly, very difficult, for any group which is persecuted seeks first and foremost its survival and the survival of the values it thinks essential. The absence of sufficient freedom of thought and action leads to a perversion of discussion so that the latter is not used to seek and express objective truth but to serve its own ends (par. 106). As a further sign of the seriousness of the Church's intention to conduct such a dialogue, the Holy See recently announced the establishment of a secretariat to conduct such dialogue between Christians and nonbelievers. It is, as we shall see, a most welcome step in the progress of mutual understanding between these two large groups of mankind. The difficulties, however, remain immense.

The Christian, however, cannot despair for two reasons. First, he must seek out his enemy to do him good, to return benevolence for malevolence. He must seek what binds and heals rather than what separates and destroys, he must know that even when he must resist the injustices of his enemy there are bounds of morality beyond which he may not go and who must never discontinue the sometimes discouraging attempt to seek peace and an atmosphere of trust and confidence. For his pains, furthermore, the Christian must be prepared like Jeremiah of long ago, to be considered himself a "traitor" or "soft" toward a hated group. At best he will be regarded a subversive whose motives will lead to "surrender" and "destruction." This, of course, is the paradox which Christianity is: "love your enemies: do good to those who hate you." Too many Christians have been imbued with the philosophy of hate and fright: destroy, hate, and put the atheist outside the human community. Too many of us have substituted the State Department and its propaganda as well as that of a certain type of crude "Christian" patriotism for the gospel. To love the enemy can scarcely mean less than to understand why they are as they are and why they act as they do.

Second, change is of the essence of every society, of every philosophy. A philosophy that does not continuously adopt itself to new conditions is doomed to death or at best, irrelevance. This has been and is historically true of Christianity as it has had to face up to the sometimes hard truths of depth psychology, evolution, pluralism and freedom, positive sciences, and the whole wealth of development of terrestrial realities. The Church today is confronted by the city of man in revolutionary change as at no previous time in history. This is true of the Church vis-à-vis communism today as well. Men do not repudiate the doctrines and dogmas to which they have sworn their loyalty. Instead they rationalize, revise, and reinterpret them to meet new needs and new circumstances. Pope John explicitly recognized this in his momentous encyclical, *Peace on Earth*, when he said:

> It must be borne in mind, furthermore, that neither can false philosophical teachings regarding the nature, origin and destiny of the universe and of man be identified with historical movements that have economic, social, cultural or political ends, not even when these movements have originated from these teachings and have drawn and still draw inspiration therefrom. . . . The movements working on historical situations in constant evolution, cannot but be influenced by these latter and cannot, therefore, avoid being subject to change, even of a profound nature. Besides, who can deny that these movements, insofar as they conform to the dictates of right reason . . . contain elements that are positive and deserving of approval (par. 159).

Both John XXIII and Paul VI, therefore, recognize the possibility of a dialogue with Marxism. The major difficulty arises when Marxism becomes dogmatic, intolerant and persecuting, and this, in fact, it has been almost since its inception. We do not wish here to investigate the historical reasons for this. Suffice it to say that the dialogue can exist only in an atmosphere of free exchange. Is this possible? It is, if, as Marxism claims, religion will, of its own weight, disintegrate in the future ideal communist state. The ideal communist society would not need religion, for the essential alienation of man by religion would be overcome in the new society. Many Marxists, in the logic of their system, ask why, then, it is necessary to persecute religion? Leave it be, they argue, for it will necessarily disappear. In a well publicized article in the *Prague Literary Weekly*, Julius Tomin, a communist intellectual, argues precisely in this vein:

> "How," he asks, "can an atheism which fears an open and honest struggle with the believer for human values possibly attract him? Such an atheism is engaged in the negative forms of religious emancipation mentioned above. The successful continuation and development of the process whereby a man becomes more fully able to participate actively in the life of a society, progressing in wisdom by learning to live consciously and effectively with mature and noble moral principles but without any need to seek the help of transcendence, is impossible unless such an atheism can be overcome. The activity of thinking openly on genuine moral and human values and a rich cultural life is the basic way to win the support of critically minded people who have not yet freed themselves

> from religion. It is the only way to strengthen and support young people, to whom religion has been something utterly foreign, against the subtle influence of contemporary forms of religion with which they are not even acquainted, much less prepared to face in struggle."
>
> "Even such a mature approach as a Feuerbachian criticism of religion has proved utterly inadequate against new forms of theological thought. Contemporary theologians escape the framework of Feuerbach so easily that they are able to use it effectively in their struggle with more reactionary and discredited forms of religion. New schools of theology are directly conditioned by the acute criticism of religion and try earnestly to transform every argument of this criticism into their own instrument. Atheism as an inseparable part of Marxism cannot accept so limited a role."

Perhaps one example is not sufficient, for a robin does not make Spring. Norman Cousins, reporting in *Saturday Review,* tells us that Premier Khrushchev listened approvingly and enthusiastically as Cousins read selected passages to him of the encyclical letter *Pacem in Terris* of John XXIII. Cousins even attests to the fact that Mr. Khrushchev was deeply moved and influenced by the appeal of the Pope for moderation during the terrible days of the Cuban crisis. Marxism is not old enough yet to realize that it has no essential quarrel with religion, for it is too akin to some of the Oriental religions at least to need to fear any danger from that quarter. Nor is Christianity necessarily opposed to Marxism as an economic system: on the contrary, it has every reason to welcome it as an ordered alternative to unbridled capitalism. The social teachings of the Church clearly attest to this fact, since she situates herself in the middle between an extreme capitalism of the pre-1929 dog-eat-dog type (from which we have happily disengaged ourselves in spite of the babblings of the right wing against the "welfare state") and the extreme statism of economic activities (from which even the Russian economy — yet alone those of the eastern satellites — is evolving).

Yet, in a true sense both the ideology of nineteenth century capitalism and Marxism is defunct. Both sides of the iron curtain, however, suffer from a common malady: materialism. Russian policy is one of a Marxist-materialist view of men and nations, yet the magnetic attraction in the Western (American) world betrays a kind of crypto-homage to the validity of its dogmas and the West's own obsession with the material factor. The problem is further complicated by the position of many Western and American leaders who continuously confuse "Western values" with a happily defunct capitalistic system which, in reality, no longer exists. This system has long been replaced by a modified system of economic collective security more in conformity with human dignity as well as with the age in which we live. Modern man has rejected both extremes of the left and of the right in economic and social reconstruction. He has, however, not done so politically, and both East and West prepare ideological war with obsolete concepts. It would not be so serious were it not for the fact that massive weapons of nuclear destruction are at the service of these ideological wars. The strategies of both groups argue beyond the true turmoil of revolutionary change present in the world today but which each uses for its own destructive ends.

I would argue that the social teachings of the Church could serve as a very fruitful basis for this dialogue with present-day Marxists, since these teachings argue beyond ideology. The trouble is that Marxists are ignorant of them, as are most Catholics, I might add. The Marxist concept of religion is the rudimental, disengaged nineteenth-century pietism so common among the Christians of that day. Christianity has come a long way from this pure engagement with the *status quo* of archaic economic and social interests of the nineteenth century, making religion truly "the opium of the people." The "good" nineteenth-century Catholic liberals (today: conservatives) practiced their religion well insofar as sacramental frequentation was concerned, but the service of social and economic justice for the brethren was not even considered a part of "worship." The same can be said today of our Latin American neighbors. The few rich (all, almost without exception) frequent the sacraments weekly but obstinately refuse any service of the brethren in just gradual taxation, agrarian reform, investment of capital at home instead of Switzerland and Wall Street.

The social disintegration of the nineteenth century with its merciless alienation and subjugation of man to the materialistic, capitalistic system was little inveighed against by organized religion. Religion, Protestant and Catholic, became a prop to the established order and, for prosperous man, a vulgar self-celebration. The contrast between a protesting atheism and a complacent Christianity is striking.

There can be, however, no living nor authentic Christian faith in God without "works of faith," and among these there is first of all that of caring for others "without distinction of persons": "thou shalt love the Lord thy God . . . thou shalt love thy neighbor as thyself" (Mt 22:36). To love one's neighbor as oneself is not confined to satisfying, by means of Catholic charities, the most urgent necessities of your neighbor. It means also and above all effectively to desire for him what we desire for ourselves: civil rights, health, education, development, civilization, and culture. It means to wage an effective war for him against the evils which we fight for our own advantage; to do our best to eliminate the great economic and social inequalities and the oppression of man by man. Unless priests get across this social message to their people as part and parcel of the Christian message, then we can simply forget about any meaningful *aggiornamento*.

To be a Christian is not purely to serve God but it is also a dynamic social ethic, a service to mankind; it is not merely a theology but also an anthropology. And although Christianity is directed to the "beyond" it nevertheless must influence our actions in the realm of the "here below" of fostering science and promoting civilization. It must give a deeper meaning to our bond with the world and with history. Solidarity with the agonies and problems of modern man becomes the sacrament of God's saving presence in the midst of the world: "I was naked and you clothed me; I was in prison and you came to me" (Mt 25:36–40). The social encyclicals of the Popes, John XXIII reminds us in *Mater et Magistra*, are nothing more than the continuity of this living voice of the Gospel applied to the modern agonies of men.

The widespread representation of Christianity as the antagonist of the communist social system, or even of the socialist organization of society, is very dangerous. It creates the impression that the Christian faith is primarily a negative and conservative force in social matters, that it is the strongest bulwark of the capitalist concept of society and the distribution of wealth. Christianity thereby loses almost all of the creative value of the social revolution that is embedded in her own doctrines.

This is unfortunate, even tragic, since the social teachings of the Church can revolutionize the world, can make the Church meaningful to modern man and his problems. She can vitally contribute to the reorganization of today's world. Yet this force can be effectively applied only when Christianity pays heed to the true causes of the social disease and fights the evil in its roots.

The natural reaction to the Church when she attempts to make Christ's teaching relevant and meaningful to modern man through her social teaching is one of disbelief and dismay. What has the Sermon the Mount to do with civil rights, urban renewal, nuclear disarmament, the UN, the economic society, immigration, internal law, peace movements, racism, nationalism and internationalism? The answer is simple: everything, for the Church's teaching on these aspects is her vital life-line for the salvation of men of *this* world, at *this* time. To misunderstand the social teaching of the Church is to misunderstand the very nature of Christianity.

The Marxists must recognize this evolution if they are to enter into dialogue with what, up to date, they have persecuted in the name of "alienation." Is such a Christianity necessarily an alienation of man from the city and task of man here below? I think not and if the Marxist is logical, he will have to admit that he is beating to death a nineteenth century carcass. There is a possibility of dialogue here which goes beyond slogans to reality and it ought not to be missed by Marxists.

But Christians ought also to realize that there is the other side of the dialogue: understanding the goals of atheistic Marxism. We must study its true characteristics.

It is clear that in the midst of this struggle for a new and better community, for a more deeply developed man, no Christian can stand aloof. Wherever a man's life, work, or dignity are threatened, Christian values are at stake. The joyful gospel of Christ has renewed man in the fullness of his human nature. When a man is treated inhumanly, Christ suffers with him.

Christians should therefore recognize that the values at stake today are truly their own, rooted in the Christian heritage. We should not be misled by the fact that they are not expressed in scholastic terminology, not even by the fact that the struggle for true values in the social order has often divorced itself from personal values which have become discredited by making religion a private affair. We are embarrassed by the self-centered values of some Christians. From the point of view of the Christian who has created a religion in his own image and likeness, the entire struggle for peace, freedom, and universal brotherhood as it is being lived and suffered by mankind today must seem utterly foreign. Christians are right to point out that those who struggle most courageously and effectively for the ideals of peace, freedom, unity, and human dignity do not always stand on the ground of Christianity. These desires and goals ought not to be superficially dismissed by the Christian with slogans and clichés about atheism. He must examine and evaluate in the light of the Christian faith as well as the teeming desire of modern man for revolutionary change.

But for the theoreticians of communist doctrine and for those who constitute the moving force of present-day communism, the perfect society of the future will be essentially atheistic. For them, the transition to a communist society will be the result not only of a certain program conventionally established by the organization of work and the distribution of goods, but will also flow from the ontological necessity of things themselves. These are the hard facts of present-day communist doctrine.

This ontology — or description of things as they are — is not a crass materialism. In understanding such a theory we must not think of an opposition between materialism and spiritualism in a dichotomy but rather we must speak of a materialistic monism, of the unity and autonomy of the empirical world by which and in which man arises as its supreme conscious manifestation.

Man thus perfects himself by working on the world in the ambit of its economic and social relations according to the laws of dialetic evolution which will eventually see the future absorb interior stages. The perfection of this future is compared by the Marxists to the light of a true intuition, that is, perfection and happiness will consist in the spontaneous and full adequation of the human person — by means of necessary relations — with which he inserts himself into total reality. Such an integration is, in reality, a communism, not an opposition or division. Submission is a liberation. The objective order brings about the maturity of the subject. Society signifies the free expansion of each individual within the expansion of all the others.

This ideal perfection will be the humanistic reduction to reality of every potential and possibilities of man which can be attained only by a historical society to which we must refer all those values which are called spiritual values.

The result is that man is neither fully conscious of his power nor can he reduce all his possibilities to practice. Either by ignorance or by the deficiency of technical and social evolution and organization — by virtue of which some usurp that which belongs to all — man is not fully realized as yet: he remains alienated. He must realize himself more fully in the plenitude of social life by freeing himself from the pressures and dominion of these alienations. The state of alienation is expressed in ideologies (philosophical, moral or sociological) which proceed to elevate to an absolute what is only a relative, transferring that which in reality is in the hands of man, to some supernatural category. Every ideology is an abstract system superimposed on man which intends to hold back the liberating revolution and which certainly attempts to retard it (by class division, by private and public divisions, by divisions between time and eternity). Against a truly human evolution, ideologies subordinate man to nature, or to other men, or to God.

Religion is one of those ideologies in that the importance and dependence of man is explained by a feigned relationship to the divine order; thus is formulated a patient submission to this superior will which offers man consolation by evasion. Religion makes man search outside of himself and this is, of course, pure illusion; it is a secondary derivation of the division of defective socioeconomic harmony. Thus in religion, there is no special value; rather it has a nefarious effect on man.

The negation of religion or the denial of aspirations to the transcendental and the consequent reduction of man to the sociotemporal life, are not, properly speaking, for the Marxists acts of renunciation: they neither believe that man does not know what he must hope for or do (as do the agnostics) nor do they deny that these aspirations have real content in themselves (as do pessimistic existentialists). On the contrary, these aspirations of man which are projected on God in an illusory manner are not in themselves illusory; they can be reduced in reality in the future ideal society which will absorb in itself the "divine values."

This new form of society has dedicated itself to a united effort toward a new humanism. Christianity, on the other hand, is not bound to a particular social system. The socialist system is one of several possible solutions to the economic problems of a state. But for us there is a catch in socialism. In contrast to the preceding social orders, socialism does not rely on religion in the process of building up society. On the contrary, it regards religion as useless, and even dangerous and harmful. The Church seems to be losing her place. A new situation is being created for the Church and Christians. For the first time in her history the Church is encountering an integral, programed atheism.

Atheism is an organic part of the Marxist world view, which is the main ideological basis of the socialist state. Marxist atheism is derived from a detailed analysis of the manifestations of religion in the nineteenth century, and its negation of religion has a predominantly social character.

This atheism has within itself its own eschatology, i.e., the final and orientational significations of man and his creation. We must judge atheism in this light since the validity of this atheistic interpretation of history and man depends on this eschatology. If we may be excused for simplifying a complicated question, we may say that it is a sort of "terrestrial messianism." It is for this reason that this atheistic interpretation can say that religion is an alienation to the degree that man can do for himself that which religion formerly did by prayer, etc. Thus religion is superfluous in the perfect communist state, since man is so totally identified with himself in his created spacio-temporal ambit. There every aspiration will be satisfied, and if desire or hope remain it will be entirely circumscribed within the ambit of the possibilities of the socioeconomic world. Not that religion which is hoped for will be realized materially, but rather that tension will cease, or better, that the disparity between objective possibilities and subjective tendencies will cease.

In its own way, Marxism recognizes, whether we like it or not, the reality of the aspirations which religion itself recognizes. Since subjectivity is something, it is a mode of reality, and every tension is toward something. Logically, if in the future society — as perfect as it can be — some aspirations are transcended, we must consider this transcendence as a human constituent and it must necessarily be admitted that objective reality corresponds to a subjective reality.

We must not approach this whole gamut of explanation in a polemic or apologetic. We must use it as a way to dialogue. The anti-agnostic bent and realistic spirit of Marxism can lead to a positive dialogue which, up till now, because of lack of sincere and open love of truth, has been impossible — as Pope Paul noted in *Ecclesiam Suam*. Precisely because they tend to recognize the fullness of human reality, we must invite them to consider this tendency to God not as an alienation but rather as a dynamic perfection of man.

We Christians sometimes see in the concept of atheism the negation of all moral and religious values. An atheist is for us a conglomerate of everything negative. In short, he is a degenerate. It is true — and an honest and sensitive atheist is able to admit it — that people have often resorted to atheism to get rid of all moral values and norms. Even today we see such cases. But such an atheism is not the subject of our present analysis. We must distinguish among the various forms of atheism. It is a gross simplification to identify atheism as a whole with its most negative form. The sweeping declaration that atheists are "beyond good and evil" is an effort to relieve us of the obligation in truth to penetrate more deeply to the precise nature of atheism and to ask if it was not we who, through our poor example as Christians, helped give rise to it. Our daily contact with various kinds of atheists forces us to recognize that Marxist atheism is not merely a biased denial of religion from a trifling encounter with some shallow-souled believer (which kind of encounter incidentally gives little witness to our faith). Rather, we are led to see that the kind of atheism proposed by the Marxists represents a struggle from a new starting point for a solution of moral problems and in fact of the basic question of life. Marxist atheism appears as a humanistic view of life claiming the whole man and seeking to solve all his problems, thus giving him a certitude and moral norm for living, similar to that found through faith.

Marxist atheism is more than simply an anti-church or anti-religious campaign. If we were to judge Marxist atheism in our country solely on the basis of its propaganda, the picture would be just as poor as would be a judgment on religious consciousness based on attendance figures at religious services. Marxist atheism is striving for a revolutionary world view, which is not dependent on its formal rejection of religion. It is trying, in the spirit of our times, to restore to people a purpose in life and to give the whole struggle of mankind a higher meaning. We cannot ignore this effort, to the extent that it is directed at human and moral progress (Cf. John XXIII, *Pacem*, par. 159).

Even more to the point, Marxist atheism makes a crushing indictment of Christians. If we examine its criticism, we can recognize that its most important argument is the fact that Christianity, during its almost two thousand years of existence, has failed to do away with poverty, servitude, wars, and social disorder. Christians have betrayed their mission in the world. They have allowed their faith to be used to support the powerful against the weak, to become a weapon against the small, contributing to their bondage. We cannot erase these facts from the history of Christianity. As a concrete example, let us cite the example of war. The Church — at least indirectly — showed the way to modern total and ideological warfare. The defense was that of the purity of religion against the heretic and infidel. The crusades were the first exercise in the concept of total destruction of the enemy for what theologians of the Middle Ages called the "common good." But whose common good, indeed? The intolerant common good of a few (Christians, or, in the Old Testament, the Jew) against the heretic and the infidel. The Inquisition, the bloody crusades, the witch hunts, the annihilation of the Cathari in Southern France, the truly total wars of religion during the sixteenth and seventeenth centuries all give abundant testimony to the beginnings of modern total and ideological wars. In the face of these facts, there can be little doubt that Christianity itself, as concretely lived, has been one of the major causes of unbelief in the modern world.

We can only learn from these past mistakes, and in a spirit of deep humility before our Father and his Son, Jesus Christ, acknowledge the guilt of past generations which clings to us who strive today to bear the joyous message of Christ. Since atheism does confront us with these facts, however, it is fully justified in standing against us.

Thus, we must strive for a deeper evaluation of atheism and its consequences. We must recognize in particular the fact that many atheists take questions of life as seriously and earnestly as we do, that they often struggle equally to subdue all that is brutal in them and to realize the deeper qualities of the human character. Atheistic efforts must be approached with seriousness and understanding. One sign of our age is that it strives for mutual understanding and sympathy. We sometimes complain about a lack of understanding on the part of an atheism. But what have we done toward an understanding of the atheism in our country? It is therefore a matter of analyzing ourselves as Christians and of divorcing ourselves from those forms of action, often identified with Christianity, which in fact, pay tribute to a past world.

Atheists, however, must recognize that Christianity is not an ideological system which alienates concrete reality. With the Church the Marxists admire and imitate the love of reasoning; but they accuse the Church of abstractionalism. For this reason, we must show them clearly and incessantly that the Church is founded in a historical fact, in the personal revelation of the love of God in Christ, and that its doctrine is in accord with the integral reality of man, that it appears as a transcendental fact beyond the variable socioeconomic structures. Christianity is not only an historical fact, it is a transforming force projected toward the future. It is not a closed doctrinal system. The Christian fact illuminates man insofar as it shows a direction, a goal and thus engenders confidence in man himself; but we must be careful not to give the impression that we can illuminate all the complications of human reality by deducing them from given principles, as if the Church or Christianity is a reasoning mechanism or computer. There are mountains of problems to be approached in humility, openness, sincerity and a willingness to learn. Among other problems facing the dialogue is the care Christians must take not to reduce the future life to an imaginative translation to heaven.

Christianity as the at least nominal way of life of almost a quarter of mankind should be leading all men toward an acceptance of everything positive in the world today, all that is born, lives, and develops under the impact of the present. John XXIII opened windows so that fresh air could blow into the life of the Church; the first encyclical of Paul VI opened the dialogue of the Church with the world. Let us not shut the windows again. Let us not break off the dialogue by neglecting the art of understanding. For understanding was the great art of "good Pope John" and the treasure he gave to an impoverished lot of Christians.

CHAPTER IV

THE CHURCH'S PRESENCE IN THE WORLD

I

We are living in exciting times for the Church. We have already begun to renew our worship, our liturgy, making it an affair of intelligent and active participation. The desire for unity of the Christian community has never been so strong, nor has it ever received the encouragement it now draws from the ecumenical movement. A deeper appreciation of the Sacred Scriptures has immensely contributed to our spiritual lives. These movements are renovations within the structure of the Church, both in its strict interpretation as the Catholic Church and, more broadly, the entire Christian community.

There is another dimension of the Church which needs to be rethought in our day. This is the dimension of the Church's relationship to the secular world and her witness therein. Since Leo XIII (*Rerum Novarum*) up to and including Pope John's two earthshaking documents, *Mater et Magistra* and *Pacem in Terris*, the Church has developed fully a whole new dimension to her being: the corpus of social thought. In our seminaries, we have treated this corpus as an adjunct "added on" to the "regular courses" in dogma, moral, Scripture, etc. This attitude, of course, not only lessens its importance but fundamentally distorts the incarnational mission of the Church. Dogma and social principles are not two entities which exist alongside of each other. On the contrary, they are two sides of the same coin. Worship of God and service of the brethren make Christianity to be what it is.

Thus liturgy, which is nothing more than "dogma prayed," in the phrase of Vatican II, can never be a simple ritual, repeated phrases and readings, but of its very nature it must be viewed as radically oriented toward daily life. There can never be any disjunction of the two. They are two sides of the same coin of worship, of the Christian life lived in Christ. The life of a Christian is the test to see if he has really grasped what God has told him in the liturgical assembly. His life is a continuation of the liturgy, a continuous offering, a sort of prolonged and vital liturgy.

We all know very well that worship has within it elements of adoration, gratitude, contrition, and petition. But what the Christian community does not seem to understand to any significant degree is that worship is also a school for fraternal service. The ancient Greek word expressed this very well: *Koinonia*, communion. This designated both communion with the Lord in the liturgical assembly and also the service of the brethren, which is only the natural outcome of our mutual commitment to and love of Christ and in Him to each other as true brothers. The great commandments of love of God and of neighbor are indivisible, and worship is the bond which makes them one. The New Testament word for love (*agapē*) is used indiscriminately for both God and man. The Church worships in order to prepare men for the service of man. The dialogue in the liturgical assembly must not and cannot go on apart from neighbor and the notion of service. To erect a dichotomy of this kind is a monstrosity and unfortunately this goes on today despite the frequentation of the sacraments. In a sense, this is the great tragedy of modern Catholicism: too long have we separated worship from the service of the brothers, from our fellowman without regard to race, color, or creed.

The situation is very serious. The mute and individual worshiper who does not realize this Christian and human solidarity and responsibility, who busily promotes his private bartering with God, is a contradiction in terms.

The vital unity of doctrine and social justice as the concrete application of doctrine in practical life cannot be overemphasized in the training of future priests and laymen. It cannot be relegated to a course or two in first or second theology; it must be spread throughout the whole of education; for our effect on the modern world will radically depend on whether we can meaningfully apply the social teachings of the Church to the world. In this corpus of social thought, the Church speaks the language of modern man, becomes involved in his problems and agonies. If the social teaching of the Church is not lived we can forget about *aggiornamento*. I cannot overemphasize the vital importance of stressing the whole corpus of the Church's social thought. The students' and the seminarians' minds must be as totally imbued with it as they are with their scholastic theology, because on this will depend whether we shall have anything meaningful to tell the world, or whether we shall continue spouting irrelevant "natural law theories" to a world which neither understands us nor is in any way attracted to us by what we have to say.

The liturgy "makes the Christian" (to use the phrase of the ninth-century French ritual); it gives him identification both with regard to his celestial calling and his earthly commitment to the city of man. In reality, the worship of God and the service of man are two sides of the same coin of worship. To emphasize one at the cost of the other is to destroy the Christian message of the good news of salvation. One cannot separate liturgical worship from social action for the two together spell the Christian total commitment. If we stress liturgy at the cost of social action, we have a kind of "transcendentalism" which has been characteristic of Catholicism of the past 400 years (as well as Eastern Orthodox Christianity). As Péguy once remarked, the reason why many Catholics do not have dirty hands is because they have no hands. The concomitant complement to the liturgy is social action; both together are the fullness of Christian action and commitment. On the other hand, if we stress social action and justice without the liturgy, we have a type of terrestrial messianism similar to that of Marxism.

It is impossible to live an authentic life of faith unless the "sanctity" of the Christian spills over into his daily life, into the workaday world of material realities wherein he lives out his commitment to Christ. The interior life of grace is, of course, indispensable. Without this, Christianity is reduced to an impotent humanism. On the other hand, some stress this interior aspect of the Christian life to such an extent that the temporal vocation of the Christian to the world is left almost unnoticed. To do this is to reduce Christianity to a barren contemplation of God with no repercussions in the temporal order. The true Catholic notion of sanctity is to respect the complex character of these two fundamental realities while trying to find an equilibrium for both. One recognizes the disciple of Christ by his external life, by his conduct and attitude in the face of all reality and existence. His faith must communicate and inform his temporal activities. We must recognize that, on the one hand, Christianity has a value in itself quite independent of its repercussions in the temporal order, and, on the other hand, that it is absolutely necessary for one to be preoccupied with these repercussions if one does not wish Christianity to evaporate, to lose contact with the concrete world of human existence. These two aspects — the divine life and temporal vocation — seem so essential to Christianity that it is impossible to sever them in any way.

We see only what we want to see and not, as should be, the total vision of faith of what the Church really is. She is always holy in her origin, her doctrine, her saints, throughout the course of human history; but she is also, here on earth, the *ecclesia semper reformanda,* the Church of sinners, of those who continuously need that conversion (the New Testament *metanoia*) of heart. To stress dogma and liturgy to such an extent that social action becomes a mere adjunct, an extra, is to deny the incarnationalism of the Church, her divine-human existence among sinful and miserable men. The Church is in the same economy of salvation as is the Word incarnate, who took upon himself absolutely everything that we sinful men are and have, except sin. Here was scandal enough, for, in the final analysis, the criteria of both Christ and His Church are not, cannot be the criteria of a human person or a human organization. In this, they occupy the same sphere of human scandal: "The Jews demand miracles and the Greeks look for wisdom, but we, for our part, preach a crucified Christ . . . who is the power of God and the wisdom of God" (1 Cor 1:23, 25).

Thus our confusion when we come to measure Christ and his Church in human categories. St. John depicts Christ's triumph when he is crucified on the Cross (the Greek word which St. John uses when speaking of the crucifixion is glorification). The Christian's real triumph occurs when he is dissolved and made one with Christ (Phil 1:23). He is most like Christ when he suffers (Gal 2:20–21); here below, there is such a bond of union between Christ and the poor and despised of this earth (Mt 25:35), that they are his choicest friends and companions—because they are the most despised (Mt 9:11).

This is the logic of the gospel. Have we as a group really taken seriously this logic of the gospels? We have always had our examples of heroic poverty in our midst: the many religious orders and others who have taken the vows, the great saints. But it is strange that when the gospels speak of the poor, the despised and the neglected, the message is for all the followers of Christ. We have simply not taken the gospel seriously on this point, yet it is clear for all to read. We have followed the casuistic moralists in distinguishing "heroic" poverty from the "ordinary" demands of ordinary Christians. The religious would practice the former and the rest of the faithful could ride along on the Christian life with considerably less. In practice, this has come to mean that poverty is something foreign to the layman and the diocesan priest. The idea would be comforting if it did not contradict the gospel. Every Christian by his very profession must practice poverty and what he has must be used in such a way as to best aid his brothers.

Only in this context can riches make any sense for the Christian. But we have gone merrily on our way with a type of bourgeois Christianity which is very characteristic of American Catholics. "The good life" is part and parcel of American (and *ipso facto*) Catholic thinking. We have managed to "baptize" this as much as possible; we have "opiumized" our consciousness by various "charity appeals," support of schools and institutions with the result that the Catholic conscience in the United States can rest fairly easy ("we are a generous Church") in the midst of forty million poor, in the face of the "other America," and in a world where half of the globe's population goes to bed hungry every night. How did we get to this point? Our pulpits have helped "opiumize" their congregations by making them believe that if they "support" their Church and various other charity appeals, they are good Catholics. The poverty of the gospels is not even discussed for fear of a "fanaticism" by those who would take the gospel too seriously.

And what of our association with the poor and despised in accordance with the gospel's logic? Is it in conformity with these social teachings of the Church? Here indeed speaks the wisdom of the world in Catholicism's midst. We cannot discuss here the utter failure of so-called conservative type Catholics to respond in any meaningful way to this essential phase of Gospel teaching. It is enough to mention the failure of Catholics in great numbers to meet the challenge of the race problems in the United States. We are beginning to wake up, but only after the Negro himself has forced us to take stock of our own Christian teachings and its connotations for race. To be close to the poor? The answer of too many Catholics to sane urban renewal was and is a massive exodus to the suburbs and the "good life," while leaving those stinking and squalid poor in their own blighted neighborhoods. Get out as soon as you can, especially if a Negro moves into the neighborhood. Panic and run, don't stay to suffer and be identified with the poorest of humanity.

Another point is that of the international community. Pius XII spoke frequently and favorably about the United Nations and its objectives, and Pope John in *Peace on Earth* made explicit reference to the United Nations as a positive embodiment of his ideal of the international authority of the international community. Many American Catholics seem to manifest a massive reluctance to endorse any form of internationalism which requires the smallest surrender of American sovereignty. A fairly sizable element of American Catholic community was never in full sympathy with this side of Pope Pius' and Pope John's thought, and it has even failed in general to become acquainted with it. Pope John's *Peace on Earth* will serve as a clear and authoritative rebuke to those Catholics who have not relinquished this false notion of exaggerated nationalism and who have thus failed to appreciate the mind of the Holy See on this highly important issue.

Let me say immediately that I do not blame those Catholics. They have simply been the recipients of a notion of religion which was restricted to sacramentalism and ritual without a dynamic orientation of liturgy and doctrine to applied Christianity, social Christianity.

But the liturgy, the announcing in word and act of the good news (gospel) and communication of Christ's saving paschal mystery would be emasculated if it does not aim at a spiritual offering and a lived gospel, to and for charity among all men, the conversion of the world, and the consecration of the whole world and its activities to Christ.

Laymen, members of God's people in full right, who have participated in the sacred mystery and who have centered their lives with Christ, dead and resurrected, at Mass, are the same members who must put the Holy Sacrifice at the center of their lives in the world, among men. They are Christ's true envoys, his ambassadors; they are the spiritual prolongation of Christ's saving liturgical mystery in the midst of their brothers in the world. In virtue of this saving liturgical mystery, they must render this earth more inhabitable, more humane, more just.

All of the modern revolutions, from a social point of view, have been conceived outside of the Church and sometimes in opposition to her: Democracy, religious liberty, the social, the psychological, the scientific revolution, women's suffrage, and finally the slave problem and civil rights. The charge is grave but can be amply substantiated. The problem for the modern Catholic is to enter into each of these fields and reap what is good and fine in them and bring the light of charity and faith to bear on them. The first stage of the rocket to fire modern Catholicism out of a Constantinian chauvinism came with modern Popes, from Leo XIII up until John XXIII. A new age, the Johannine era, is upon us for the future and it promises such magnificent spiritual fruits that one dare not at this moment try to enumerate them.

Pope John fully recognized this problem in his magnificent and revolutionary encyclical, *Peace on Earth.* Both this encyclical and *Mater et Magistra* must be read to see all the social connotations which flow from the direct profession of the Christian faith. For the social teaching of the Church is not a sort of afterthought of the body of Christian doctrine; on the contrary, it is the living, vital, and dynamic embodiment of Christian teaching to the basic and human problems here below. General teachings are of little value unless they are brought to bear on the dirty and agonizing problems of real men in a real world in the course of human history. When the Church attempts to do this, she immediately becomes relevant to man's problems and *ipso facto* repugnant to many Catholics who have conceived of the Church and religion as a kind of ivory tower, as a purely individual confrontation between "sweet Jesus and me."

II

At the end of the first session of Vatican II the essential

mission of the Church was formulated by Cardinal Suenens as pointing in two directions. Her mission was within the Church itself by constantly reforming and redefining her methods for each new generation of Christians. The eternal message of the good news of salvation must, of necessity, remain always as her Divine Spouse gave it when he founded the Church. The cultural forms into which that message has been poured must continuously come under the scrutiny of the Church to see if they communicate the purity of the Savior's mesage to her children of this age. If not, then it becomes her solemn duty to embody this message in different cultural forms more in conformity with the mentality and understanding of men today. The task is very delicate, indeed, and it is the solemn duty of the Church, and her alone, to approve of these new forms. But the Council has made one thing very clear: no cultural expression of Christianity, be it Roman, Greek, or Jewish, can ever exhaust the Christian message, much less can it be the eternal and unchangeable robe or form in which the good news of the Savior is forever and unalterably entombed. It is this work about which the Council is so diligently at work. In the words of John XXIII to the assembled Council Fathers:

> It is one thing to speak of the substance of ancient doctrine contained in the deposit of faith and another of the formulation in which it is vested. We must give great importance to this form and work patiently, if necessary, at its elaboration; we must have recourse to ways of presenting things which correspond better to the teaching authority of the Church which must be, above all, pastoral in nature.

There is another dimension of the Church which is also an essential dimension of her being: her relationship to the world. It is a presence of witnessing Christ in the midst of men as the "sign raised up among the gentiles." This dimension of witness or presence to and for the world is not simply a complementary aspect of the Church's mission on earth; it is a basic dimension of her very nature that is in question. One is struck by the complementary aspect of both of these dimensions of the Church —

her internal nature and her witnessing Christ to the world—for one exists, in a sense, for the sake of the other. One cannot be understood without the dynamic presence of the other. Her internal structure, her discipline and rule, which are continuously reformed and renovated under the guiding hand of the Holy Spirit, proclaim more clearly and more purely God's word to men, both within and without the Church proper. She is the proclamation of Christ and the continuation of Christ's salvific mission in space and time. She is the continuing incarnation of Christ among men in this double dimension within and without the Church. The grace of God in Christ as king and priest is not something superimposed on the world by the Church. This kingdom of Christ must extend itself day by day in the world during the course of human history. In this sense, the Church is beyond her members; she is the heavenly Jerusalem descended from heaven and dwelling among men, more particularly among those who have accepted her and believe her but also among those who are visibly outside of her. Only in that way can she merit the exclusive title of "Catholic" Church among men. This Word of God in Christ thus exists in time through the presence of the Church.

The development of science and technology has changed the course of human history not only in a quantitative measure (the production of more commodities and material transformations) but also qualitatively. The human condition of over two thirds of humanity has been changed radically during the past fifty years, more radically than at any other period of recorded history. And the one-third of the human race as yet unaffected by this revolution now at least has within its grasp the means for changing their lot which has been that of the majority of men from the very beginnings of recorded history. Man is no longer the passive agent of nature in the forms of floods, and famine; he has become and continues to become more and more the lord of his history in his passage from a primitive being to a human culture and environment. The world and human history lie today in a context wherein man has become its center and guiding agent. The world exists today in its own right. Here lies the great originality of Vatican II as opposed, say, to Vatican I. The Church is no longer concerned with the periphery of her relationship to the world as was Vatican I. Such questions as the relationship between science and faith, between evolution and Scripture, or even between Church and state were — and to a much smaller degree continue to be — important questions for the Church. But the frame of reference has changed from that of an external relationship (Church *to* World) to that of an interiorized relationship of this dimension to her very nature (Church *within* the World). The problem today is much more radically posed than in times past since it involves the relationship between the civilization constructing the modern world and the evangelization of that world by the Church.

One of the fundamental characteristics of this new world is what Pope John called "Socialization" (*Mater et Magistra*, pars. 47–49). He used this term in the sense that modern sociologists use it, namely, as a type of global and universal interaction of persons and things. The concept involves a complicated intertwining of many and varied relationships in the economic, social, and technological fields. It affects all nations and peoples; and men have thus become socially dependent on each other in a great number of institutions and associations. These relationships might be called elements of fact which have united mankind in a unity never before thought possible. All of these technological, economic, and cultural changes have been of great service in advancing civilization, that is, in bringing about a greater sharing on a global basis of the common patrimony of all men by all men.

History has known nothing of this intensification which began with the industrial revolution and continues today at a breathtaking pace. Socialization was and continues to be a great blessing for men, since it has brought in its wake the fulfillment of many human rights which had been unfulfilled from the beginnings of recorded history because of the primitive conditions of society. In a very real sense, man has been, in fact, freed from the slavery of fate by socialization. Health and group insurances have freed him from the instabilities of health; social securities, from the economic infirmities of old age; automation, from the slaveries of back-breaking toil; communications, from the restrictions of time and space. The modern phenomenon of socialization has permitted man's spirit to grow and expand to encompass the whole globe. He is, in short, in control — at least potentially — of his destiny under God.

The secular world has come into its own possession, into its own right without the need of tutelage of the Church. It has become fully secular in the original vocation given to man in Gen 1:8: "Dominate the earth." Henceforth the basic elements of human society — physical subsistence, economic structure, cultural and artistic organizations, care of the sick and aged, aspirations toward ever more perfect social justice, efforts toward peace and fraternal solidarity among men — are fully the right and responsibility of this newly born world. Formerly — for lack of anyone else — the Church was forced to do all these things herself, erecting thereby a whole complexus of organizations and structures which were secular in scope. This phase of her history is now both unnecessary and harmful to her mission to a world in the process of secularization and humanization. All these efforts and aspirations which have been championed by the Church for over a thousand years have become the common patrimony of humanity as such and the content of its fondest hopes throughout a world still in the feverish drive toward its fulfillment. Man has become conscious of the laws of his own nature insofar as he has discovered, and continues to discover, the laws of nature itself. Man confronted by nature becomes more human through the growth of science, reason, culture, and society. This secularization of the world by man is a direct development of Christian revelation itself. Accordingly, against all pagan religions, the world as God's eternal creation has been handed over to man, to his experimental science and technical might. This is the clear teaching of the author of the book of Genesis who sees all creation as good because it comes from the omnipotent hand of God, and for whom man, as God's lieutenant, is to continue this act of creation in the world which has been handed over to him. In a very true biblical sense, man's work on the world is a command from God and, as such, man cooperates with God in the continuous act of creation, understood in a secondary but real sense.

That is why the Church has always condemned any kind of Gnostic-Manichaeism which would consider the world and material creation as the work of evil. Christianity has long been confronted with such a temptation. The first heresy that was condemned by the Church was precisely Gnosticism. The Nicene Creed contains the unambiguous phrase that God is the Creator of all things, "visible and invisible." Consequently, and this will have momentous consequences, Christian man alone is capable of giving a fully human meaning to the material universe. Pope John's view of the human city is a daring one: the human community ought to be, or at least Christians ought to strive to make it, an imperfect but real reflection of the kingdom of Heaven; where justice, peace, freedom, and love are perfect. The Pope put it this way in *Peace on Earth:*

> Human society, Venerable Brothers and beloved Children, ought to be regarded above all as a spiritual reality: in which men communicate knowledge to each other in light of truth; in which they can enjoy their rights and fulfill their duties, and are inspired to strive for moral good.

This slow maturing of the world which has now come into its own right has been accomplished, for the most part, outside of the Church and her influence and sometimes in spite of her opposition. In its early origins, this revolution was even thought to replace God in a blasphemous manner. A terrestrial messianism would replace Christian messianism; and man, so long alienated from himself, would achieve his own kingdom here on earth by building the city of man and rejecting the false hope of religion, the opium of the people. These violent episodes were and continue to be most painful, for these essentially humanistic dynamisms, such as Marxism, contain a great kernel of truth and have acted as the painful first movements of the birth of the new era for man and for the Church. To be completely absorbed in condemning the errors therein contained is to lose sight of the direction in which such humanism is taking man. It will be the most sacred duty of the Church to fully understand these movements and aspirations of men and, by entering them, fulfill them in the process of modern evangelization.

In understanding these movements, we begin to see the grave paradoxes and ambiguities of science and technology. They can be used for good, or for unprecedented evil by man to the point of self-destruction of the human race as we know it today. Without a spiritual direction from *within*, these forces will follow their own dynamism, which inevitably leads to egoism, nationalistic aggrandizement, conflict, and, ultimately, self-destruction. That is why it is so vitally important for the Church fully to comprehend this juncture of history, this appointed time given by God to the Church, perhaps for the last time. If the Church fails to implement and inspire this newly developed and developing world, it might well mean the end of man and his aspirations.

The Council says with regard to the laity that:

> Today they are called by God that by exercising their proper function and led by the spirit of the Gospel, they may work for the sanctification of the world from within as a leaven. In this way they may make Christ known to others, especially by the testimony of a life resplendent in faith, hope and charity. Therefore, since they are tightly bound up in all types of temporal affairs, it is their special task to order and to throw light upon these affairs in such a way that they may be made and grow according to Christ to the praise of the creator and redeemer (*Constitution on the Church*, par. 31).

Only man has an absolute end given him by God himself. But neither does this mean a regime of simple empirical concessions and practical opportunism. This autonomy is nothing which man — or the Christian — can see or discard as he sees fit. This autonomy means that earthly or terrestrial realities do have a final value and end in themselves; yet their autonomy and finality are secondary to the final end of man which is God. Yet they are not simply and purely means. It is for this reason that the satisfaction of the needs of this world and the sustaining of the world's hopes denote a fundamental and real human dignity, a very high moral value. As the Council points out once again:

> The faithful, therefore, must learn the deepest meaning and the value of all creation, as well as its role in the harmonious praise of God. They must assist each other to live holier lives even in their daily occupations. In this way the world may be permeated by the spirit of Christ and it may more effectively fulfill its purpose in justice, charity and peace. The laity have the principal role in the overall fulfillment of this duty. Therefore, by their competence in secular training and by their activity, elevated from within by the grace of Christ, let them vigorously contribute their effort, so that created goods may be perfected by human labor, technical skill, and civil culture for the benefit of all men according to the design of the Creator and the light of His Word. May the goods of this world be more equitably distributed among all men, and may they in their own way be conducive to universal progress in human and Christian freedom. In this manner, through the members of the Church, will Christ progressively illuminate the whole of human society with His saving light.
>
> Because of the very economy of salvation the faithful should learn how to distinguish carefully between those rights and duties that are theirs as members of the Church, and those they have as members of human society. Let them strive to reconcile the two, remembering that in every temporal affair they must be guided by the Christian conscience, since even in secular business there is no human activity that can be withdrawn from God's dominion. In our own time, however, it is most urgent that this distinction and also this harmony should shine forth more clearly than ever in the lives of the faithful, so that the mission of the Church may correspond more fully to the special conditions of the world today. For just as it must be admitted that the temporal sphere is governed by its own principles, since it is rightly concerned with the interests of this world, so also that unfortunate doctrine that attempts to build a society with no regard whatever for religion and attacks and destroys the religious liberty of its citizens, is rightly to be rejected (*Ibid.*, par. 36).

Pius XI once called this "political charity" which is exercised not sporadically by any individual, but by the assured justice and charity which comes from socialization in all of its forms. To feed the hungry, for example, even while forgetting all the rest, inclusive of God, is an important action in and of itself. This action has a moral character all of its own because it responds to the innate demands of human dignity and compassion. History shows well that the Church through the centuries has served humanity in carrying out these highly moral social functions. But this was essentially a substitutional function of the Church until such time as the world could develop into its own fulfillment. In centuries past, the efficiency of human groups was as yet inadequately constituted. The diaconal duties of the Church as give by the apostles to the first deacons must now be seen as something essential to the structure of the Church. Her essential function must always be to serve men, to save them by her service, not to dominate and direct man's activities. The diaconal duties of "serving tables" must be seen as a transitional and tutorial function through the ages until such time as man comes into his full growth.

The twentieth-century Church no longer need take a direct hand in the ordering and directing of civilizations and the promotion of the good of peoples in the form which she has followed for the past 1,000 years. Her role must change in order to be efficacious in the world of our day, and if she is to fulfill her essential mission of announcing the good news of salvation to the world within the world. She must introduce the evangelical ferment into these new civilizations, into these new structures of humanity which in the past were more or less the patrimony of the Church but which today have become the patrimony of the human race. It is no longer the duty of the Church directly to feed the hungry, to elaborate economic plans, to introduce social security services, to undertake agrarian reforms, to institute cultural developments in the underdeveloped countries. Rather, she must collectively pledge her faith, her hopes, her charity in the service of the construction of today's fraternal humanity. She has not to construct (to use some familiar words in Christian circles) or initiate a "Christian World," but she must christianize the world as it develops.

It follows that in her wholehearted fidelity to her divine nature and to God's word, the Church's commitment has to be made according to the laws of earthly realities. When God speaks to man, he uses human speech and adopts himself to human conditions. So too the Church will not proceed to carry out her task simply by easy applications and adaptations as types of abstract deductions; she fulfills her mission by means of her concrete knowledge of men, of their problems, and of their history. To use the now famous expression of Pope John XXIII, the Church must attentively and affectionately observe the "signs of the times" of and in a world in revolutionary motion.

It is precisely at this point that we find the vocation of the layman in the Church within the world. The apostolate of the layman must be that of the necessary link of the Church in and for the world. This apostolate is not to "convert" the world from the outside, leading it to the Church (as was formerly thought in the nineteenth and early twentieth centuries). Rather, it is to penetrate the world from within by understanding modern humanism and by causing Christian faith to become its ferment through the layman's action on the world. In a true sense, this apostolate spells the success or failure of the present mission of the Church to the world. The layman must enter fully into all the ramifications of the temporal order if he is to bring out the image of God contained in the world. In the true biblical sense of the word, the layman is God's lieutenant in creation, prolonging creation in accordance with the image of God given to him in faith. His proper mortification will be continuously to purify his own intentions, and not to despair when, at times, he sees no direct connection between his work and the kingdom. If faith is demanded in God's mysteries, for man can never fully comprehend them, so too is faith required in restoring and fermenting the temporal order with the Christian ideal. In this sense, the layman partakes of the work of the Church in its full and cosmic sense. Taking encouragement from St. Paul (Col 1:15–20) who originally had this gigantic and total vision of the Church and of Christ's triumph through it, a layman's proper vocation is to bring out this Christlike image by fecundating the new humanism with the Christian *Weltanschauung*. It is necessary to return a total view of the living Church and, above all, to a total vision of the Church's task in the world where everything has a religious, though not necessarily supernatural, meaning: A total vision of the Church in its supernatural as well as natural commitment. By failing to emphasize this total and dynamic structure of the ecclesiastical community, the layman has seen his function within the Church as peripheral and obscure.

III

We have situated the Church to the world in fact and in doctrine. A close relationship to the world — indeed presence to and in the world — pertains to the natural right (and therefore, responsibility) of the Church. This right is concretely realized by the witness of laymen who fulfill themselves and their function in the Church by engaging intimately and daily in temporal life. This right of the Church in its mission to the world is traditional doctrine; its far-reaching implications are more and more evident every day as the new world of man expands all of its potentialities. This right is central to the argument of *Peace on Earth* by Pope John XXIII and to the teachings expressed by Vatican II in the *Pastoral Constitution on the Church in the Modern World*. In both documents we find discussions of the dignity of the human person, family structures, the right to economic, cultural, and moral goods, social justice with its ramifications, the community of peoples, war, and peace. All these human situations call for the presence and action of the Church from within. These earthly structures and values call for the active presence and fermentation of the evangelical message both of individual Christians and of the Church herself as the community of Christians. The Church has not the mission of directing and managing these institutions, of "controlling" them by domination and power. The Church is not even to chaperone them by a certain type of paternalism. Rather the Church's mission is to be there, to be present — even while respecting the autonomy of earthly realities. The Church is to be in the world as witness of the word of God among men and as the yeast of the gospel. This evangelization will depend on the active presence of Christians within the development of the modern world.

Thus the Church cannot and must not seek to dominate in the worldly sense of the word, using its prestige in competition with political forces and temporal societies, fearfully hanging on to supplementary institutions which were formerly the source of much social prestige for her. Her evangelization must be one of complete service by active presence and witness to the values of the gospel. It is as the bearer of this evangelical message rather than as a society armed with rights and power that she discerns, amidst the rapid evolution of the world, those ferments which contain Christ's promise of a more abundant life among men in search of new economic and cultural foundations. Thus the Church, bearing the burden of the needs, hopes, and sorrows of all peoples, will be at the service of men. In this she follows the example of Christ who came to serve, not to be served. In this way, she manifests her poverty and her enormous capability for good by witnessing Christ *within* the world, within the new humanism.

In the words of Pope John to the Council Fathers the message of good news of Christ is the eternal and abiding truth of the Church. This witness to God's word among men by the Church is an essential dimension of her being as given to her by Christ himself. Yet the cultural embodiments of that message have and must continue to change as the history of man continuously changes. This adaptation of Christ's message to new cultural expressions is the continuous task of the Church, the *ecclesia semper reformanda*. Happily, this task has been seen clearly by John XXIII and the great majority of the fathers of Vatican II. The task now is to make the laity see vividly this dimension of the Church. Laymen must realize that their natural talents, their creative potential, are not only given to individuals for their personal benefit and salvation, but are by their very nature social. They concern men in society insofar as the social life of man forms part of his very nature. Man is not an individual; he is a person, autonomous in his inner freedom but dependent on other men for his personal growth and development. Thus, to take one example from among many, it is not simply a man's work alone which may find material disposed toward grace; a civilization itself based on man's work presents resources capable of reflecting the kingdom of God. Man's creativity and participation in divine causality has an essential social dimension and it develops more fully as man develops himself more fully in history. This view of man's developing social nature is of capital importance in the modern world where "socialization" in the sense given it by Pope John is the major and universal phenomenon in mankind's evolution. That is what Origen long ago saw when he said that the Greco-Roman civilization was an "evangelical preparation." So too the values of the modern world — order, justice, human rights, cultural and moral riches — are considered by Pope John and must be considered by the Church as forerunning signs, as predispositions for the diffusion of the gospel in the modern world.

In the actual makeup of mankind, in the modern worldwide extension of social, political, and cultural values, in the universal consciousness of the rights of man, there are today, just as in the early Roman Empire, possible resources for pre-evangelizing, for constructing the kingdom of God in the modern world. These contemporary values call for rethinking the traditional structures in which the evangelical message has been carried and for a bold attempt by the Church to re-incarnate this message into the new framework of the modern world.

No doubt these values have been and will continue to be ambiguous, contaminated in fact by error and sin; it was the same at the time of the apostles. Yet we are in a time of transition where new methods and attempts at accommodation must be made; there will be some mistakes but progress has never been achieved without a willingness to risk some danger of error. And the need for this dynamic *aggiornamento* is urgent in the Church today. It is true to say that, after necessary purification, these values of the modern world are of great importance. For example, the solidarity between men, created by labor organizations and commercial necessity, is an admirable predisposition toward evangelical fraternity; it can become a potent preparation for implementing this evangelical fraternity into the modern world. Furthermore, the anguished aspiration of men and of peoples for peace and for its international adoption is a great predisposition toward the hopes of men of good will.

These, of course, are only some of the many situations where the presence and action of the Church are called for by the needs, hopes and even the despair of modern man. They are the meeting places for the dialogue between believers and unbelievers. If the Church does not discern these capacities for grace in the present transformation of humanity, it will lose the providential opportunity which history is offering for the earthly construction of the Kingdom of God. She must see, in this transformation of human civilization, the emergence of truths and values contained in her deposit, which up till now have not found their true reality nor their full expression in the lives of all men. These are the truths and values which lay implicit in the human capital of this Christian doctrine. Modern values and aspirations would simply remain "pagan" and untransformed if they were not to become the material for a witness to faith, for the work of Charity. Through the Church in the midst of the world, Christ is present not only in the inner life of each Christian, but also in the history of mankind on its way toward final consummation in Christ.

Thus, the Church is missionary not only in space by implanting herself in new lands, but also in time by sanctifying the civilizations and cultures which develop from century to century within the territorial expansion of mankind. Today we have arrived at a solemn moment in this history. This is the chosen time, the biblical *kairos*, for the Church today.

Hence, we define the presence and action of the Church in the world not only by the subjective virtues of individuals but also by the objective content of the structures of human society, while respecting the distinction between the construction of the world and the advent of God's Kingdom and while affirming the transcendence of grace. In this consisted the revolutionary views of Pope John XXIII in both of his encyclicals, *Mater et Magistra* and *Pacem in Terris* as well as his intention in calling a general council of the Church. It will remain for the future to see whether the Church shall have lived up to this cosmic and profoundly spiritual vision of Pope John and Vatican II.

CHAPTER V

THE PROGRESS OF PEOPLES AND THE CHURCH OF THE POOR

I

Each social encyclical of a new Pope seems to create a minor crisis in the Church for the rather evident reason that outspokenness on the part of the highest teaching authority to concrete problems of men is a shock. For some strange reason many in the Church — they are neither few nor recent — are Docetists or Manichaeans. They cannot bring themselves to take the Incarnation seriously, for then they would have to take man seriously in all of his agonies and joys (*Pastoral Constitution on the Church* par. 1). If we seriously believe that Christ became a man, then he touches and brings to healing every man and each problem and joy of every man. The Greek Fathers called this the "Law of the Incarnation" whereby the Savior truly touched our bodies and souls and thus brought to total man his healing and his salvation. For man's salvation cannot be abstracted from the concrete life of man but is rather intimately united with it. The Docetist or the Manichaean does not and cannot believe this but is trying to find man's salvation in "spiritual" things or in another world "out there." He cannot take seriously the identification of Christ with every man (Mt 25:34–40), especially the poor and destitute; nor does he grasp in a personal, real way that the peacemaker and the doer of justice is thereby the intimate friend of Christ (Mt 5:1–10).

It is commonly assumed today that the Church is undergoing a very deep crisis. This is substantially correct but not for the rather superficial reasons sometimes given. Some would divide the Church into "conservative" and "liberal" wings. The former is characterized by a holding on to past cultural expressions of Christianity, and the latter by an openness to change and accommodation to the world as we live and experience it today. The problem in the Church today is much deeper than nomenclatures or clichés; it is not a question of changing one vocabulary for another, nor of substituting the vernacular for Latin, nor a question of clerical celibacy or even of birth control. These questions, of course, are of great interest to the Church, but they do not attain the essence of the problem. The essential problem is our conception of God himself. We can know God only as he manifests himself to a man at a particular time and within a particular culture — and in no other way. There are indeed eternal verities, but these are not experienced as truth, as a living message, unless they receive flesh and blood among a particular people in human history and in temporal reality. This was the law of the Incarnation in the Gospels, where the Incarnate Word was born in a particular time, from a particular woman, in a particular nation with all its time-conditioned manifestations. This "Law of the Incarnation" is the continuous way in which God reveals himself to us — as the *Constitution on the Church* of Vatican II reminds us — and this is the only way we can find Christ today: in the face, in the encounter of our brothers as they live out their concrete existence in the world of today.

It is precisely here that we have a deep schizophrenia in the very heart of the Church. There are very many in the Church who wish, somehow or other, to find God "out there," in a sanctuary, in a church, in St. Thomas, etc. They simply do not see the relevance of the world of our day; they wish to regress to God "in himself," contemplating the eternal "verities in themselves." This, as Marx saw long ago, is an escape from the realities of man with whom, by the Incarnation, God is forever implicated. It is pure illusion, where we substitute God for man and thus escape concrete man with his agonizing problems.

The other conception of God follows from this "Law of the Incarnation," where God can be found only when we have found man, where God manifests himself to us in the face of the problems, agonies, and joys of our brothers. They thus become for us the hidden revelation of God's presence among men. God has become visible in Jesus Christ, the man, just as he has become visible in the extension of his body — all men. The comparisons which Paul and John use to describe this unity are very realistic; "one body," "his members," "the vine and branches," "life in Christ," etc. In the new dispensation, to be implicated with man is to be implicated with God.

It is precisely to this question that Pope Paul VI in his most recent encyclical letter *Populorum Progressio* addresses himself. It continues the work of his predecessors from Leo XIII to John XXIII in the matter of social justice, who unanimously proclaim that man has been called by God to live in a total fashion: social, political, cultural, economic, moral, and spiritual. We cannot abstract the "spiritual" and say that it can live and exist independently of the rest. This would result in an eviscerated Christian existence, since God has made man as a total whole and his total vocation is to be what God has created him. This includes the economic as well as the political, the social as well as the spiritual. To belittle any is to belittle man and to belittle man is to commit blasphemy. That is why the Popes — and Paul here continues their voice — are so adamant on *social* justice since it is man who is at stake. Following the very examples of the Incarnate Word, the Church cannot be disincarnate without betraying her mission. This comes through strongly in Paul's encyclical on the development of peoples (cf. par. 12, 14, 15–16, 21, 28, 32, 74, 80–81).

As Paul notes, practical application of the supreme Christian virtue of love must become manifest in economic and social fruits among men. The Christian vocation can only be a vocation of the whole man as an incarnate spirit (par. 14). The Pope voices eloquently true Christian personalism, maintaining that the divinely given vocation of every human being is to develop himself totally, humanly and divinely. This Christian vision of man does not deny but rather absolutely demands a true humanism (par. 16) which is open to the transcendent action of Christ. The Pope's stand here is a direct response to Marxist humanism which is closed to the higher synthesis of both a human and divine order. Christian humanism is one of hope and of openness to its absolute future where man's works and man himself is not lost but purified and transformed by the action of Christ's resurrection (par. 28).

To work for more human conditions among men is, in reality, to work for the extension of the Spirit of Christ in extending the implications of the Gospel itself into the world of men (par. 32). Those who turn themselves to the poor and the destitute, in reality are turning to the very voice of Christ who is identified with the poor and the weak (par. 74). Thus, a universal fraternity is born from these efforts of more social justice among men with the result that it leads to peace and harmony among men, a premonition of the perfect peace and justice to be established when Christ comes to inaugurate the final kingdom (par. 80).

All of these exciting challenges of the Pope point to the central theme of the encyclical: we must take the Incarnation to its logical conclusion in and among men.

II

Certainly one of the most important aspects of *Progressio* is its attempt to update papal teaching, particularly in its international aspects. This solicitude has never been completely lacking in papal social documents but neither has there been a concerted and developed effort to give the social teachings their international connotations. The present encyclical letter closes this gap (cf. pars. 3, 5, 48–49, 58, 62, 77, 81).

It is a truism to claim that in the world of today, the rich grow richer and the poor either remain poor or are actually becoming poorer (par. 47–48). Seventeen percent of the world's people consume somewhat less than 80 percent of its goods while the rest must subsist on what little remains. The United States consumes fifty percent of the world's wealth and controls eighty percent. It is true that poor countries are poor partly because of their own lack of development and technical know-how, their background of colonialism and consequent retardation of industrial development (monoculture, etc.) (cf. par. 7), the manifold abuses of failure of distribution of the riches which are present in these countries (par. 9). All of this remains true, yet throughout the globe runs the revolutionary idea that a country or a people need not be poor or starving; that there is enough technical know-how to insure each man on the face of the earth a decent living and a comfortable existence (par. 1). Poverty, it is said, is not of itself a revolutionary factor; it is when people realize that poverty is not inevitable that revolutionary expectations arise throughout the third world of our day. This fact alone should impose a moral obligation on all men of goodwill, and particularly on Christians, to do all in their power to attempt to alleviate the miserable, radically inhuman situation of the world's poor. For this, the Pope reminds us, there must be a more reasonable distribution of the world's riches to the world's poor in the next twenty–thirty years. Somehow or other, means must be found to stem the flow of greater riches to those already rich and of greater misery to those already miserable. What we need, once again in the words of the Pope, is a complete change from the economic system which presently runs the finances of the world and is, to a very large degree, directly responsible for the imbalances of rich and poor today. It is this alone which can eliminate the humiliating paternalism of "gifts" and "grants" from the rich to the poor. This might well be necessary as an emergency measure for the next few years but in order to attain the essence of the problem we must re-examine the very principles of economic justice pertaining to the world community as such and go on to establish political and economic structures capable of bringing about radical reforms of social justice.

The greatest obstacle to this type of thinking is the fact that to date in matters of social justice we as Catholics have been too inhibited in applying the social principle of the Gospel to our own nation. As in other areas, an exaggerated concept of national sovereignty is present here, with little taste or courage to apply the reality of social justice on an international plane where today it is most needed (par. 62). The idea of patriotic chauvinism has blocked our view of the "Catholic" needs and necessities of the human family and of each human being in particular. After the crash of 1929, Americans were faced with this problem as millions were on relief and other millions on subsistence incomes. The laws of Social Security, Workman's Compensation, Widow's Survival, and a whole list of other social legislation remedied to a large degree the great imbalance between rich and poor and, at least to a certain degree, effectively redistributed national income so that the majority of Americans could live in economic and social decency. In fact, it has become evident through the application of Keynesian economics that the more wealth people have, the more things they can buy, and this in turn creates more employment and wealth. We must now start thinking of how we can apply this very same principle on an international level and what *demands* of social justice are to be met in the process. The essence of the social doctrine of the Church is the same in both cases, namely, that each poor man on the face of the earth has the absolute right from God to receive these goods and in the amount necessary for his sustenance as a human being. To deny this either explicity by laying an exaggerated emphasis on "property rights" (par. 22) or implicitly by invoking "national sovereignty" is to deny the most basic of man's rights which come from God himself. It is the very idea which must be developed on an international scale and which the Pope here attempts to cope with.

John XXIII reminded us in *Pacem in Terris*: "Beginning our discussion of the rights of man, we see that every man has the right to life, to bodily integrity, and to the means which are necessary and suitable for the proper development of life; these are primarily food, clothing, shelter, rest, medical care, and finally the necessary social services" (par. 11). The land of the earth has been given to all men for their use as incarnate beings and as such, the primary right of usage is superior to even the right to private property. Because men are incarnate spirits and must use material goods, all things have been created for their well-being. The goods of this world correspond to man's needs, and to live as a human being and to perfect his person, man must make use of them. And if he must, he has a right to do so. This right of usage is the fundamental and primary right with regard to material goods. The right to private property is secondary and derived, and it exists so that an order might be established in which the right of usage is assured. Thus the rights of nations or of private property or of any other subdivisions of humanity are all secondary to this. The principle of subsidiarity must be applied within any one particular country but not to the point where fundamental human rights of other men cannot be honored. Too long have we applied this fundamental principle of social justice to an individual nation and not to the international community as such (pars. 22–24).

It must then be clearly stated as a principle of social justice that the riches of any one nation must in justice be related to the international common good of humanity, from which no individual nation can disengage itself under any condition. No nation can use its property purely "as it sees fit" or to the detriment of other nations or to the common good of the whole of the human race. It should be evident from all this that no nation has any right to riches which far exceed minimal needs when a great mass of men go without the very necessities of life (par. 49). The principle is so very simple and evident that it comes as a shock to Christians and as a terrible scandal to the mass of humanity which is both poor and non-Christian. There ought to be worldwide bodies with sufficient authority effectively to distribute the world's goods according to priorities (par. 78). This is not a matter of idealism, but a demand of strict social justice. It is only in speaking in such terms that poverty on a global basis can be effectively challenged and overcome. Nothing less than this will do from a Christian point of view. An economic democracy of this kind will vindicate the economic rights of all men and bring to an end a regime of monopolistic privileges of the few rich who compose less than twenty percent of the world's population while consuming over eighty percent of its wealth.

The principle of redistribution of wealth ought to be such that it guarantees to each individual nation *as a right* from the world community sufficient resources to permit its citizens to live a decent human economic and social existence; in its turn, the recipient nation would contribute according to its own means and resources. The terms of exchange would be submitted to objective and strict terms of social justice in conformity with the well known adage of social justice: to each according to his needs and from each according to his abilities. This principle runs throughout the encyclical (pars. 1, 6, 15, 17, 20, 22, 28, 26, 34, 39, 47, 65, 79). This principle is diametrically opposed to an atomistic economic system, what Pius XI called "an international imperialism of money," still influential today (par. 26).

The distress in the present economic and social sphere on an international plane is not dependent on any particular individual or group of individuals, but on a whole system of capital which runs its own course with its own laws and which can be cured only at its root cause: personalizing that which has been brutally and inhumanly depersonalized in this system. The distress proceeds from a profoundly dislocated social and economic structure on the international scene and as such has an inhuman effect on the human person — particularly the poor since it reduces men and nations to a means for economic progress and gain and profit motive. We shall have to find equitable and efficacious means to promote this international social justice, *founded directly on the principle of the solidarity of the human family and on no other* (cfr. pars. 3, 5, 44, 48). The Pope is speaking, then, not of "foreign aid" or "charity" (even if they are needed as a stop-gap for the present), but of strict social justice. Otherwise, it will become simply impossible to stop — let alone alleviate — the slide of the poor nations into further degradation. This calls for an international taxation on actual income, to be redistributed internationally as regard to actual need. This would not be very difficult since we already have the needed machinery in the United Nations, and a progressive income tax would meet the international emergency in a just and satisfying way. The obstacle here is the cancer of excessive nationalism which is surely most difficult to break down (pars. 61–62).

Thus, each nation has, in social justice, the absolute obligation to contribute to the international society according to its abilities. It is obvious that the poor nations will profit from this redistribution. However, in the long run, by making these poor countries productive and consumers, the whole international community stands to gain. At present market values, not human values, rule the system of international exchange. This permits and even promotes economic imbalance in the world between the rich and the poor. Thus it prolongs the terrible scandal of a minority of a rich eighteen percent of the world consuming more than eighty percent of the world's total wealth. From a humanistic point of view, this situation is intolerable, and from a Christian point of view it is simply criminal. Thus because the market value is low, some countries will actually burn food while others actually starve to death. Other nations produce luxury items by the billions of dollars worth (last year, teen-agers in the U. S. spent over 15 billion on absurdities from rock and roll to falsie bras — more than the whole GNP of Southeast Asia) while millions of other men go without the very essentials of life. This results when a capitalism motivated excessively by a desire for profits is applied on a worldwide scale. This, according to Pope Paul, must be radically broken if the world's poor are to attain any kind of human dignity in our age.

Thus, the principle of subsidiarity and the right of usage and of property need be conceived along international lines. We need a much broader concept of social justice than one which is applied only to national entities. The reason is quite simple: the human race is of greater dignity and prior to any nation. If we readily accept the responsibility of redistributing income by progressive income taxes for the nation, why should it appear so strange to apply this same concept to the international community, which is prior in dignity to individual nations? The concept of social justice is the same in both cases.

Of various solutions to the equitable distribution of wealth on an international basis one is that of a "world fund" (pars. 51–53), preferably administered by an international body to eliminate all dangers coming from political and economic pressures exerted by the rich nations. The Pope gives no practical means of implementing this fund. Perhaps some sort of international tax could be imposed on the vast amounts of luxury items coming from the rich countries or perhaps upon arms shipped internationally. Taxation on such shipments of international goods would be fully in the competence of the U. N. as an effective international organization for peace — or, at least, it should be. Perhaps this would be one way to bring about what John XXIII so ardently hoped for in his encyclical, *Pacem in Terris*:

> Today the universal common good poses problems of world-wide dimensions, which cannot be adequately tackled or solved except by the efforts of public authorities endowed with a wideness of powers, structure and means of the same proportions: that is, of public authorities which are in a position to operate in an effective manner on a world-wide basis. The moral order itself, therefore, demands that such a form of public authority be established (par. 137).

For our present purposes, such structures already do exist in the U. N. (for instance, the International Bank) if only men have the moral courage to use these structures more widely and contribute to them justly.

This doctrine concerning international social justice is not just a creation of idealistic Christian thinkers. It was developed as far back as St. Thomas Aquinas and developed by the Popes from Leo XIII to Paul VI. Paul's encyclical simply follows *The Constitution of the Church in the Modern World* of Vatican II, which also developed this whole idea. Here are some relevant passages:

> The right to have a share of earthly goods sufficient for oneself and one's family belongs to everyone. The Fathers and Doctors of the Church held this view, teaching that men are obliged to come to the relief of the poor, and to do so not merely out of their superfluous goods. If a person is in extreme necessity, he has a right to take from the riches of others what he himself needs. Since there are so many people in this world afflicted with hunger, this Sacred Council urges all, both individuals and governments, to remember the saying of the Fathers: "Feed the man dying of hunger, because if you have not fed him you have killed him." According to their ability, let all individuals and governments undertake a genuine sharing of their goods. Let them use these goods especially to provide individuals and nations with the means for helping and developing themselves (par. 69).

An emphasis on the international implications of the Church's social teaching is intrinsic to the very concept of man, for human justice contains the very seed of internationalism in its very definition. As Pope Paul remarks, "Today we must recognize that the social question has become worldwide" (par. 3). The Pope bases the whole doctrine not exactly on revelation but on the much more widely accepted social principle of the brotherhood of man under the common Fathership of God. This principle elicits a response in most theistic religions, and even in atheistic circles it finds an analogate in the principle of socialism: "brotherhood" (par. 44). Proceeding from the natural basis of human justice to its supernatural culmination, the Pope never cuts off from the dialogue those who accept only the first part of his foundation for brotherhood. The Christian simply has the added motive of Christ's supernatural love for all men, and his commitment to his brother men in Christ simply increases his responsibility. The Brotherhood of all men must take on concrete expessions of love in increased aid to the poor nations, and this *obligation* rests on the wealthy nations both *individually* and collectively (par. 44, 49).

Paul's teaching here is not new for the Christian, since the doctrine of men's international and social responsibility is nothing more than the explication of what is clearly implied in the Christian dogma of the solidarity of men. It is a truth which socialism — in its own, sometimes twisted way — saw and continues to see. Hence, when the Pope is accused of "socialism," the charge is substantially true since Christianity is essentially socialistic internationally in its concept of universal brotherhood. This international morality must be emphasized today in Catholic circles and plunge the layman into working for deep-seated reforms that are urgently needed today: "They [Catholic laity] will certainly desire to be in the first ranks of those who collaborate to establish as fact and reality an international morality based on justice and equity" (par. 81). This work can only be done in collaboration with all nations because the problem is not national but international (par. 77) and its greatest enemy is nationalism (par. 62).

"The way to Peace lies in the area of development" (par. 83). With one stroke the Pope cuts through the semantics of the "cold war" and its clichés to the very heart of the true problem alive in the world of 1967. The conflict today, the greatest danger to peace today, says the Pope, is not "Communism vs. freedom" or "free enterprise vs. socialism" or any other slogan so often heard in the western and eastern propaganda machine: it is the problem of poverty, of the rich and the poor nations where the fate for the future survival of mankind resides. Western Christians have been taught — almost to the point of obsession and automatic reflex — that the greatest danger to peace is Communism. This the Pope flatly denies (he makes only one small reference to this problem in par. 11). The real danger comes from the egoism, greed and consequent materialism of the developed nations, both east and west (par. 41). Here indeed is a revolutionary view of the modern situation, and it will not please many Christians of the right who see the incarnation of all evil in

Communism. If anything, the Pope goes out of his way to stress the principle of universal human solidarity and to blast the extremes of economic liberalism, of lust for profits (pars. 26, 58) which presently rule to great extent the international market. The way to peace and security in the modern world is for the rich to do more to help the poor nations (pars. 5, 44, 49, 54–55, 76).

The lesson is here for all to read. The rich must aid the underdeveloped countries of the world economically and socially in their revolution for true freedom from want and misery. Without this, "political freedom" is just a mockery (par. 54). This is the true revolution alive in the "third" world. Perhaps this is the only lesson to be learned from the tragedy of the Vietnamese War, where we have already spent more than fifty billion dollars for war and death and a pittance for economic and social aid. As if to make his thought crystal clear on this subject the Pope says bluntly: "But let everybody be convinced of this: the very life of the poor nations, civil peace in developing countries, and world peace itself are at stake" (par. 55). Perhaps this is the clearest analysis of the Vietnamese conflict to date.

Paul writes: The world is sick. Its illness consists less in the unproductive monopolization of resources by a small number of men than in the lack of brotherhood among individuals and peoples (par. 66). The Pope thinks the work of helping emerging nations is so important that he praises those governments which have made military service optional so that young men can devote themselves to the true work of development and peace (par. 74). Pope Paul even goes beyond the principles set down for conscientious objection in the *Pastoral Constitution* of Vatican II (par. 79c), or perhaps it would be better to say that the Pope here dramatically concretizes the principle set forth in that revolutionary document.

In this respect, then, the dialogue between believer and unbeliever can be most fruitful indeed for they are both working for man for a more humane milieu as well as for world peace.

The unbeliever (atheist) has no reason to suspect that the

Christian has ulterior, proselytizing motives behind his desire to ameliorate a particular political, economic, social, or cultural system. There is no such thing as a "perfect" society here below; but there are means and ways to promote man's dignity and welfare, to redeem them from the slavery of alienation and the forces of un-freedom (par. 21). There is no such thing as "Catholic" politics or "Catholic" economy or "Catholic" internationalism. There is only man as the supreme value here below and it is man himself, who is the middle and essential term in the dialogue between believer and unbeliever (*Ecclesiam Suam*, par. 25). The Christian cannot put man and his faith outside the concrete world with its real problems and urgent needs (par. 1, 3, 5). He cannot escape into a false mysticism or an illusory transcendentalism where the affairs and needs of his brothers are left "here below" (par. 13). Such a view may well be neo-platonic but it certainly is not Christian. Christian man does indeed look beyond the terrible realities of the here below, but not to evade them or to rend them illusory; rather, by loving and serving man, he prepares for his Lord's *Parousia* in the very act of love for his brothers (par. 79). One thereby avoids both pernicious errors against Christianity; disincarnationalism and terrestrial messianism (par. 11). Social organization indeed has its proper autonomy; it is indeed distinct and independent of the hierarchy of the Church in the exercise of its proper domain; it can never be separated, however, from God and his intent for man (par. 13). The universal value here below can only be man and it is for him that social organization is created, not man for social organization. As Christians, we are always men, and human dignity and endeavors must always be of supreme importance. In this endeavor and in this sense, there can be no radical division or difference between believer and unbeliever — and this must be kept firmly in mind if there is to be a true dialogue between the two. The Christian religion today — as a "sign of the times" to use the famous words of John XXIII — means meeting God and Christ in the face-to-face encounter with man in the world (par. 1).

III

It is evident that the whole encyclical is one great appeal for the poor throughout the world. The Pope is merely following the Gospel injunction that as often as we serve the poor and destitute in this world we mysteriously but really are serving Christ himself. The major motif of Vatican II and of Paul's *Progressio* is *service* to the needy of this world (par. 1) This was forcefully brought out in Vatican II's *Constitution on the Church* (par. 7):

> Just as Christ carried out the work of redemption in poverty and persecution, so the Church is called to follow the same route that it might communicate the fruits of salvation to men. Christ Jesus, "though He was by nature God . . . emptied Himself, taking the nature of a slave," and "being rich, became poor" for our sakes. Thus, the Church, although it needs human resources to carry out its mission, is not set up to seek earthly glory, but to proclaim, even by its own example, humility and self-sacrifice. Christ was sent by the Father "to bring good news to the poor, to heal the contrite of heart," "to seek and to save what was lost." Similarly, the Church encompasses with love all who are afflicted with human suffering and in the poor and afflicted sees the image of its poor and suffering Founder. It does all it can to relieve their need and in them strives to serve Christ. While Christ, holy, innocent, and undefiled knew nothing of sin, but came to expiate only the sins of the people, the Church, embracing in its bosom sinners, at the same time holy and always in need of being purified, always follows the way of penance and renewal. The Church, "like a stranger in a foreign land, presses forward amid the persecutions of the world and the consolations of God" (par. 14), announcing the cross and death of the Lord until He comes. By the power of the risen Lord it is given strength that it might, in patience and in love, overcome its sorrows and its challenges, both within itself and from without, and that it might reveal to the world, faithfully though darkly, the mystery of its Lord until, in the end, it will be manifested in full light.

The text of the Council is quite clear in its implications for the life of the Church. Christ accomplished his work of salvation while on earth in poverty and persecution. It follows that the Church can do no better than to follow the example of her divine Founder, even in its visible manifestations.

But what is the Christian duty to the poor? Where is the source for his mission? How can he help? Pope Paul's encyclical is a direct answer to these questions.

Because the Christian view of poverty and the poor emanates from the Bible, God's Word, a true Christian compassion for the poor must begin in a revitalization of the evangelical doctrine of poverty in Christian lives. This message is seen most obviously in the life of Christ. The poor Christ of the Gospels, after all, was the true Son of God, but he humbled himself to become a man, taking on all that we are, save sin. To show man the way, he took upon himself all the consequences of the human condition, including miseries of poverty and death. By becoming poor and a man of suffering, he has saved us from sin and eternal death. He has given us hope and life both on earth and in heaven. The importance of his mission is obvious, but is it not indeed interesting that he first revealed the presence of the messianic time of salvation to the poor?

Christ's poverty and his life among the poor are intimately tied up with his whole life, and his actions and words form the Christian teaching on the world's poor. Christ's teaching has a double view. First, the poor are the living image of Christ: what a man does for the poor and deprived, he does for Christ himself, and what he refuses to the poor, he refuses to Christ. Second, the poor are truly our brothers, our equals before God. Since these two concepts are basic to a Christian view of poverty, they must be examined in more detail.

Christ's intimate identification with the poor in the New Testament is not altogether new. The Savior simply continued the tradition of the *anawin* of the Old Testament: broken by poverty and oppression, the poor and humble were purified by their complete and exclusive dependence on God alone. In this view, the rich man was in danger of committing the greatest of all sins, that of pride; through pride, his wealth and power alone became his strength, his confidence, and his security. The poor, then, were a symbol for the rich man: if he wished to be saved, the rich man had to view his goods exclusively as a *service* to the poor and depressed. The poor man's exclusive and complete dependence on God was a living symbol to the rich; the symbol taught him his dependence on God, but also the common stewardship of wealth which was to be used for the service of his brothers.

The *anawin* were thus the material and symbolic poor. The Fathers of the Church never tired of repeating that only by using one's good for the service of the brother can the rich man even hope to escape the denunciations contained throughout the Gospels. Although nothing could be clearer in the biblical texts, nothing is so little preached and practiced today in affluent America. Christians have made poverty a special vow, enjoined on those in the religious life (excluding the diocesan clergy, of course), and the laity enjoys comfort and convenience, unperturbed by the fact of poverty. This situation coincides with the spirit of the world which has made vast inroads into the Christian churches, yet the gnawing fact remains that it is a diametric contradiction to the gospel. At best, American Catholics are faced with a neglect of the Savior's words, and at worst, a perverted accommodation of the Christian community with the spirit of the world. The obligation of poverty is revolutionary, because it is contrary to the spirit of the world where the man of wealth and power is the ideal. Yet this gospel message represents the authentic contradiction of the cross, of the absurd, but redeeming Christianity which St. Paul preached in the epistle to the Corinthians.

While the poor are the image of Christ, they are also our brothers, our equals before God. The foundation of man's fraternity is the communion in Christ, the divine *Koinonia*, and through that divine communion, he shares all things with God and with his brothers. The early Christians understood this so literally that they put all of their goods at the service of all others so that no one would be in need. Perhaps their social organization was poor, but they understood clearly what we today have forgotten: Christianity is a spiritual and material sharing of all things with our brothers in love. The primitive Christian community, then, stands as an everlasting sign to all ages as well as an authoritative rebuke to modern collective and individual selfish materialism which sugarcoats a flabby religious ritualism. The reminder of St. James is here pertinent: "Religion that is pure and undefiled before God and the Father is this: to visit orphans and widows in their affliction, and to keep oneself unstained from the world" (1:26). The poor man is Christ; Christ suffers in his poor. The poor man is a true, real brother. Can I refuse my brother anything when he needs me, when he suffers, must I not move heaven and earth to help and feed my beloved brother?

This idea of sacrifice and poverty for the Christian is a major theme of *Progressio* (pars. 4, 9, 12, 18–19, 21, 41, 45). It is evident that the Pope's travels put him into direct contact with the poor and that he was shocked to see the extent of human degradation throughout the globe (par. 4). His journey to India in particular must have deeply moved the Pope in a country where it is conservatively estimated that literally millions die each year of starvation and where other millions are on a near starvation diet.

The poor of the world will no longer submit to this miserable condition because of "fate" or because "it is God's will." This is a bad interpretation of God's will for men and the Pope bluntly tells us so (pars. 9, 12). The will of God is that man live in human dignity and to do this he must absolutely have a minimum of economic and social goods as well. The bane of the developed world (East and West), is that it is obsessed with the material factor, or what the Pope calls materialism (pars. 17–18, 41). The Pope's intent here must be understood very clearly. He does not, by materialism, mean material goods themselves, for he is at pains to show that these are absolutely necessary for human and humane existence. Materialism is the spiritual greed of those who already have so much, who are not only not willing to share their wealth but who simply wish to increase it evermore. It is this greed — which can infect the poor as well but is more evident in the rich — that the Pope continuously refers to. Thus Christians — and all men, if they wish to have peace — must have a *metanoia* or a change of heart based on fraternity, love and a spirit of poverty in the evangelical sense of the word. This is a *duty* on the part of the rich, not an "act of charity" out of their superfluity (par. 44). They must sacrifice themselves in this endeavor with more personal endeavors, more taxes for the poor, paying more for products from the poor countries (pars. 41, 47, 61). The Pope leaves no room for doubt on this point. It is not optional on the part of the rich and, if they refuse, the wrath of God is upon their international greed and selfishness (par. 49). The Pope describes for us in graphic terms the poverty in the world around us so as to disturb our consciences (par. 45), and he encourages newsmen to do this in season and out of season (par. 83). One need not give a great commentary on this. It is evident for all who wish to see.

The gap is widening: The rich grow richer and the poor poorer (par. 9). A bishop of one of these poor countries recently told me: "My people live not only on poverty but in permanent misery." This poverty brings about all types of human sufferings. The first is the nagging, painful hunger in the pit of the stomach which can never be satiated, day or night. In 1965 alone, some thirty-five million people (among these, millions of innocent children) literally starved to death on this globe. Poverty brings diseases that cannot be cured, because there are no medical facilities. Illiteracy abounds in these lands, where the great majority can neither read nor write (par. 35). This poverty breeds slums that make Harlem look good by contrast, whether we call them slums, bidonvilles, or favelas. It breeds crime and vice on a scale that would stagger any civilized human being. Poverty in these countries means that most people will die before they reach the age of forty and that death will be a sweet release.

Cruel irony enters when we realize that for the first time in human history, we have the technical know-how to wipe out all poverty from the face of the earth. What is lacking is not the resources or the money to do so, but the will on the part of the wealthy peoples of the earth to do so. This is a fact. In 1967 the Congress of the United States grudgingly gave 1.8 billion dollars to strengthen the weak countries, and only after earnest pleas from the President and many brutal arguments on both floors of Congress. Yet a military budget of seventy-one billion dollars, to be used for destruction, death, and if necessary, nuclear holocaust, was approved in a matter of minutes with no debate. We have already spent fifty billions in Vietnam, more than half of all the aid we have ever given since World War II to *all* the nations of the world.

The Church must manifest her preferential love and prophetical witness for the poor in concrete ways in order to benefit the great masses of poor all over the globe. The world today expects more from the Church than mere expressions of love or enunciations of general principles; it asks for tangible and concrete proof of this love. The whole Church must take a stand, clearly and courageously, in favor of the poor every time they are victims of any injustice. This evidently implies a more forceful stand on racial discrimination, medical aid for the aged, urban renewal in all of its forms. Thus her solicitude for social justice in concrete examples will become a proof of her love for the poor. She — and by "she" I mean the whole community of the faithul, lay and clergy alike — must rebuke public authorities when they fail in their obligations to take the necessary measures to solve or alleviate the most urgent social problems of the day.

The Church must continually remind herself and all men that the rich have no special claims among the people of God, except that they have been given a special obligation, by virtue of their wealth, to be servants of God's poor. They themselves must be poor in spirit, and this attitude should characterize all of their actions. The Church has a heavy responsibility to remind the rich that unless they are poor at least in this sense, their chances for salvation are very slim indeed. The poor belong to the Church in their own right, as born citizens of God's Kingdom who have a first claim to His mercy and love. In the Church of God, they have the primacy of honor. The Church must always uphold this hierarchy of spiritual values, not only because her Divine Founder did so before her, but also to neutralize the idolatry of riches, which in so many ways dominate modern society.

IV

One of the more striking aspects of the new encyclical is its frank socialistic tone. As we have said, outside of one reference to that humanism based on "a materialistic and atheistic philosophy" (par. 39) there are no renewed condemnations of Communism or socialism. This follows the lead set up by John XXIII and by Vatican II of trying to go beyond ideological clichés to the reality of the matter at hand.

Change is of the essence of every society, of every philosophy. A philosophy that does not continuously adapt itself to new conditions is doomed to death or, at best, irrelevance. This has been historically true with Christianity when she had to face up to the sometimes hard truths of depth psychology, evolution, pluralism and freedom, positive sciences and the whole wealth of development of terrestrial realities and the city of man in revolutionary change as at no previous time in history. This is true of Communism today as well. Men do not repudiate the doctrines and dogmas to which they have sworn their loyalty. Instead they rationalize, revise and reinterpret them to meet new needs and new circumstances. Pope John explicitly recognized this in his momentous encyclical *Peace on Earth*, when he said:

> It must be borne in mind, furthermore, that neither can false philosophical teaching regarding the nature, origin and destiny of the universe and of man be identified with historical movements that have economic, social, cultural or political ends, not even when these movements have originated from these teachings and have drawn and still draw inspiration therefrom . . . The movements working on historical situations in constant evolution, cannot but be influenced by these latter and cannot, therefore, avoid being subject to change, even of a profound nature. Besides, who can deny that these movements, insofar as they conform to the dictates of right reason . . . contain elements that are positive and deserving of approval (par. 159).

Both sides of the iron curtain, however, suffer from a common malady: *materialism* (*Progressio* par. 41). Russian policy is based on a Marxist-materialist view of men and nations, yet the Western

(American) world betrays a kind of crypto-homage to the validity of these dogmas by its own obsession with the material factor. The problem is further complicated by the position of many Western and American leaders who continually confuse "Western values" with a happily defunct dog-eat-dog capitalistic system which, in reality, no longer exists. This system has long been replaced by a modified system of economic collective security more in conformity with human dignity as well as with the age in which we live. Modern man has rejected both extremes of the left and of the right in economic and social reconstruction. But man has not done so politically, and as a result both East and West prepare ideological war with obsolete concepts. It would not be so serious were it not for the fact that massive weapons of nuclear destruction are at the service of these ideological wars. The strategies of both groups argue beyond the true turmoil of revolutionary change present in the world today but which uses for its own destructive ends.

With this said, the Pope's view throughout the encyclical is a global view of fraternity, where all men are responsible for other men, where no one must be permitted to lead an inhuman existence and where human solidarity becomes efficacious especially in the redistribution of wealth on an international scale. To be quite frank this view draws its inspiration from socialism. But this should not startle us, since the major premises of economic internationalism are implicit in the Gospels. We have come full circle from Leo XIII to John XXIII. In *Rerum Novarum* Leo XIII condemned every form of socialism, attempting to exorcize the capitalist system of its blatant injustices. Pius XI (*Quadragesimo anno*) made qualifying distinctions within the socialist camp between atheistic socialism (Communism) and more or less economic socialism. The Pope admitted that there were many similarities between the Church's social thought and this latter form of socialism. Yet cooperation was not yet possible because of the latter's anti-religious bent. With John XXIII (*Mater et Magistra*) and Paul VI (*Progressio*) we have a fully accepted socialism within their doctrine which is open to cooperation and fraternity with all men of good will. None are rejected *a priori;* only those who refuse to respect the freedom of conscience of all sides are to be counted out of the dialogue. As a matter of fact, both Popes John and Paul not only start from a socialist critique of society but use these principles as an open attack on an atomistic capitalist system still pregnant in some circles. It is a rather phenomenal evolution of Church social teaching on the modern world. The present encyclical is evidence of this. The Pope speaks of "planning" as an absolute necessity by governments if aid and projects are going to be channeled properly for the good of the people (par. 50). This calls for more or less effective and strong action on the part of the governments of these developing countries and thus to a more or less concentrated state socialism, at least for the present difficult time before complete industrialization. The Pope is emphatic that whatever the economic system chosen, it must be chosen freely by the countries themselves (par. 54) and not forced on them by the rich countries. Political pressure by rich countries to adopt a given economic system is to be emphatically condemned (par. 52) as a gross interference in the freedom of the developing countries to develop in their own ways. The whole of the encyclical is based on universal human solidarity and fraternity (pars. 1, 6, 15, 17, 20, 22, 27–28, 34, 39, 42, 47, 65, 79, 86). It is what the Pope calls a Christian or "complete humanism" (par. 42) or a "transcendent humanism" (par. 16). It is based on man's openness to God and the higher life of God in Christ. What is this humanism which the Pope describes throughout his text?

Man has been created in the image of God and thus, like God, he makes progress in history and culture for his own perfection. He is, as we have already seen, God's lieutenant in creation directing and ordering creation for his own good and his own perfection (par. 16–17). Vatican II in its *Pastoral Constitution* follows biblical teaching on the activity of man on earth. God is mingled in human affairs and unless they are built and done under his direction and will they are nothing (Ps 126:1–8). With the New Testament, we see a fuller picture of human values considered from the point of view of God's intentions: the Word became flesh (Jn 1:7) and after his death took his human flesh into heaven with him and it is not to be separated from his person again. Pain, sickness and death have been given a redemptive role in the Christian context (Rom 6:58); marriage, the most fundamental of human institutions, is raised to the dignity of a sacrament (Eph 5:22–23); indeed, creation waits for the redemption of man and in the meanwhile is in pain of growth and travail (Rom 8:18); peace, joy, concord, and justice are the fruits of the Spirit and the expected qualities in each Christian life (Gal 5:22); they cannot remain individual or personal, but must first go out to the mystical Body of Christ (Col 2:17–20) and then to all men if possible (Rom 12:17–18); all human reality falls under the spiritual dichotomy of "flesh-spirit" in the Pauline sense of these words; this means that all men can and must serve Christ or be opposed to him. The epistle to the Ephesians is clearly concerned with a redemption which goes beyond the salvation of individuals (Eph 5:19; Col 1:9; 1 Cor 2:15); it is a Christian anthropolgy of the whole of creation, inclusive of the world of men and their values. Thus, in capsule form, we see that God, the Lord of History, has given a value to the realities of this world and to man.

Thus Christian faith is no excuse for escaping the world and its problems — but is rather the greatest incentive: out of love for men to be engaged in the world, for men. It is God's will which is revealed to the Christian as he engages himself in the world at the service of man where he is both subject and object, where he questions and receives a response in the works of the world as well as having and possessing a fundamental meaning for the world. Thus, for the Christian, his faith is a type of three-way dialectic between himself, God, and the world. In this context, Vatican II and Pope Paul could view man and the world in a certain optimism where "his defects are explained, while at the same time his dignity and destiny are justly acknowledged."

V

The Pope's teaching on the concept of private property is traditional, but he gives it a different stress in his document (pars. 22–24, 48–49). Emphasis is not on private property, although this is not absent; but rather upon the social function of private property. John XXIII had already emphasized the social name of private property. In the teaching of both John and Paul it is clear that the right of use is prior to and conditions the right to private property. God has created man as a body and a soul, an incarnate being, and, as such, man has a natural right to use the world's goods for the conservation of his life, the fruition of his talents, and the protection of his health. This right precedes the right to property, and in traditional Catholic social thought the right to property is derivative, or a concretization, of the right of usage. In other words, the right to use material goods is fundamental and primary, while the right to own material goods is secondary and derived.

The right to property is a means to an end, and it is therefore subordinate to the right of usage, the end in itself. Since every means is relative, the doctrine of the absolute right to private property is a grave social aberration. Clearly, then, private property must ultimately promote the right of usage. The Pope points this out in strong language when he calls for necessary agrarian reform (par. 24). In the same paragraph he scathingly denounced the rich few of under-developed countries who put their money in foreign places (Wall Street, Switzerland) instead of re-investing in their own countries, even if they will not make such a great return on their money. These citizens thereby destroy the right of usage for the many while exaggerating their own right to private property. Property is always a social responsibility (par. 3) and it must be used to promote the general welfare.

Paul's emphasis on the right of usage does not change or supplant the natural right to own private property, although some persons have made such a conclusion after a rapid reading of his encyclical and of Pope John's *Pacem in Terris*. A closer examination, however, will show that this interpretation is not correct. On the contrary, the right to private property is more important today than ever before, and Popes John and Paul want to expand the concept of private property to include recent developments. Their argument rests solely on traditional thought. In short, they want to show that private property is a relative right and not absolute, as the nineteenth-century Manchestarian liberals maintained.

Pope Paul sees the superfluous wealth of the rich as putting an obligation on the rich nations to give to the poor (par. 49), since God intends the goods of the world to be used for the welfare of the whole human family (par. 48). There can be many ways of doing this, but the Pope sees a valuable contribution to be made by increased taxation of the rich for aid to the poor, price stabilization for basic commodities from the rich countries as well as more personal sacrifice on the part of the peoples of these rich countries (par. 47). Naturally his recommendations strike some wealthy nations and individuals as idealistic even "communistic" nonsense. It is no wonder that the *Wall Street Journal,* in commenting on the Pope's encyclical, *Progressio,* called it a "baked over Marxism" precisely because it was unable to understand the social nature of goods and capital in the world as a function of the solidarity of all men.

Exaggerated individualism and conservatism (ironically called liberalism in the nineteenth century) has traditionally blasted all social reforms with bromides and specious arguments about freedom from interference and the all-pervading "creeping socialism." Ironically the abuses of laissez-faire policies (conservatism) both necessitated government intervention and cleared the way for Communism in the nineteenth century. Numerous social problems calling for government regulation were the direct result of laissez-faire policies. Granted, for instance, that I can do as I please with my property, then naturally I can shift the location of my plant without regard to employee dislocation; I can fire and hire without regard to collective bargaining; I can engage in high real estate speculation and in a host of other activities which result in social harm. Discrimination against Negroes around the world caps a long list of abuses resulting from an exaggerated view of the sanctity of private property.

In conjunction with this critique of private property, the Pope attacks "liberal capitalism" as the ruling force in the international system of the economy (pars. 7, 26, 34, 52, 54, 59, 63, 70).

The capitalist system has in fact built up the modern industry of the West. It has extended man's dominion over matter. It has truly changed the face of the earth in such a way that man is no longer dependent on the elements of nature for his sustenance; he can control nature for his good to the point where famine, drought, and over-population are becoming less and less a danger. The technology this system has developed is truly astounding in transportation and communication, making the world not only smaller but also widening man's perspective beyond this world to space and beyond. These are the undeniably good consequences of the capitalist system in the West. Yet we must also recognize just as forcefully the terrible abuse of man which has also flowed from this system. The nineteenth-century dislocation of man within society is a terrible fact, and our present civilization in the West was built on the broken bones of the millions of overworked and abused human beings. To a great degree, the civilization we have today has been built on the inhumanities dealt to poor people for over a hundred years. In the economically underdeveloped world, the situation is very serious today. This becomes evident in the case of China. Once humiliated by Western imperialism, she seeks now to displace this influence with her own hegemony in Southeast Asia. In the African states we have more of an emphasis on modernization for the purpose of self-identification and national unity. There is little self-identity in African states and because the artificial boundaries set up by Western colonialism and the cultural chaos which resulted from detribalization of the Africans have kept the African peoples from realizing their own potential. These all have had a disturbing effect on the traditional tribal unity and form of life of the Africans almost without exception. This, of course, is not to bring a value judgment on these aspects of cultural forms as opposed to those introduced by the West; it is simply to note a fact which becomes more evident every day as violence and disruption increase in the African states.

Yet, this subject of social dislocation caused by modern industrialization goes beyond our immediate objective. We shall only note here that any economy — Capitalism, Socialism, and Communism — shall have to determine for each respective system its effects upon the human condition and dignity of man, the power it exercises over their lives as well as its equitable distribution of the produce of labor, before the Christian can ever approve of cooperation with such a regime of production.

Pope Paul VI in his own critique of capitalism recognized this direction and orientation of capitalism itself. It must be noted that he refers to "liberal" capitalism (par. 26) or the type we have described above with its driving and determining factor being that of profit and gain. This can never be accepted by the Christian — or by any true man — since it dehumanizes man by making him a means to an end. The Pope criticizes private ownership as an *absolute* right since it is clear in traditional Catholic social thought that the state may take over any or all major industries if the common good demands it. There is no such thing as "absolute" right here for there is but one absolute on earth: that is man and everything else must be arranged so as to create a humane and human milieu in which man can grow as a person. If it is neccssary to socialize various industries, then the state not only can but *must* do it for the greater good of the many.

Although the Pope does not treat it directly, there is another problem which moral theology must grapple with in the concrete, that is, the question of nationalization of industries by poor countries without compensation. This is not a theoretical question since many of these corporations and monopolies were established by force in colonial and neo-colonial times. This is especially troublesome when it is realized that these corporations have already reaped their investment many times over. Is it permitted

— morally speaking — for a country simply to nationalize them with little or no compensation?

The Pope warns the developing nations not to make the same mistakes in moving into the twentieth century as did the developed nations (par. 34). An economic system which crushes the many in favor of the few can never be allowed, since the world is composed of men of infinite dignity who cannot be used as means to an end: industrialization. " . . . every program, made to increase production, has, in the last analysis, no other *raison d 'être* than the service of man" (par. 34). Such progress is not just economic (the mistake in the past of both East and West) but social, moral, cultural, and spiritual as well. In their desire for the "economic break-through," there is great danger that the developing nations might resort to totalitarianism as did *both* Communism and liberal Capitalism. The Pope's condemnation of both systems is abundantly clear from the text. This is brought out in Par. 25 where he calls liberal capitalism a "neo-colonialism," in the form of political pressures and economic suzerainty aimed at maintaining or acquiring complete dominance. Here the Pope's words seem to me to be directed to the U. S., which controls some eighty percent of the wealth of the world. The Pope fully recognizes this (par. 59) and, as a way out of this nefarious system, he calls for the establishment of "general norms for regulating certain prices, for guaranteeing certain types of production, for supporting certain new industries. Who does not see that such a common effort aimed at increased justice in business relations between peoples would bestow on developing nations positive assistance, the effects of which would not be only immediate but lasting?" (par. 61). What the Pope is saying is that such structures would at least break the stranglehold of the present international system and thus better the economies of those who are dreadfully dependent on the rich nations for their very survival. The Pope also observes the actions of capitalists at home and how they act when they go abroad to invest their money (par. 70). At home they are held in check by social laws and anti-monopoly regulation. Abroad there are no such restraints for poor countries submit to basic indignities because they desperately need what little they can get. As a result wealthy corporations and nations have only to threaten to remove their investment in order to get whatever they wish. It has not been beyond the rich countries to send troops into these poor countries (under various pretexts) in order to save these investments. Many suspect that an economic motive was the main reason for U. S. intervention in Guatemala (1955) and in the Dominican Republic (1965). Perhaps the Pope's vision of humanitarianism is utopian (par. 79). Yet, the Pope can, like Abraham, hope against hope and if nothing else, tell these people that in the long run, it will be to their own advantage to truly help these people. For if the present system continues, disaster will strike all indiscrimately.

It is here that the Pope deals realistically with the situation as it is. He openly discusses the possibility of revolution (pars. 29–31). For the first time in a pontifical document, the possibility of violent revolution is faced and — under certain conditions — accepted. This is something new in encyclicals. Pope John, to be true, had seen this possibility (*Pacem*, par. 162). There the Pope spoke in favor of gradualism, since revolution can often lead to more evil than existed in the first place. But what is to be done in those cases where the ruling oligarchies refuse to move at all? Too often in the past, rich nations, and among them we must sadly note that we have been numbered, have placed weak countries in the dilemma where they must yield to the economic and political goals of the wealthy nations or resort to revolution. This dilemma, says Pope Paul, cannot be eliminated unless there are "bold transformations, innovations that go deep. Urgent reforms should be undertaken without delay" (par. 32). Yet what is to be done if even this modicum cannot be accomplished? The Pope gives a startling answer — even if he gives it indirectly: in such cases, revolution of a violent nature can be justified. "We know, however, that a revolutionary uprising — *save where there is manifest long-standing tyranny which would do great damage to fundamental personal rights and dangerous harm to the com-*

mon good of the country — produces new injustices . . ." (par 31). What is to be done? The radical suggestions of the Pope — massive technical and economic aid from the rich countries, concentrated social direction from the governments of the developing countries, agrarian reform, a strong arm on exploiting capitalists in the developing countries — is the only solution to the impending danger to world peace. Otherwise, there will be revolution all over the globe which in its own turn can lead to world war itself. The choice belongs *both* to the rich countries and to the developing countries themselves. There simply is no third option.

VI

There are some other aspects of note in Paul's encyclical which are also important. Contrary to traditional encyclical letters, *Progressio* is very specific in its analysis and in its recommendations. This is true for two reasons: one is that, as we have said, the Pope has received such a mandate from Vatican II itself (par. 1). There would not have been any need for further general principles outlining the problem of poverty in the world of our day. The whole fifth chapter of Section II of the *Pastoral Constitution* had already done this. It remains true that although in becoming specific, the Pope does not enjoy the charism of infallibility; yet, if he were not to do so, not to engage the Church authoritatively in a specific direction, the social teachings of the Church would remain unconcretized and in the final analysis, disincarnate from the "joy and agonies" of modern man. Secondly, the Pope speaks for the countless millions of the world's poor and, as such, must announce to the world the direct causes of this poverty without which the poor will simply become poorer while the rich will become, in their communal greed, even richer. The situation of the poor is so serious — and is becoming ever more serious with each passing day — and the consequent danger to peace so great, that the Pope had no choice but to be absolutely blunt on these problems. The only way to dodge what he says (or to explain it away) is simply to ignore the encyclical.

Its language is so straightforward that it lends itself to little explaining away. One can see this by the many times he uses the word "urgent": "This teaching is important and its application urgent" (par. 3). "The Church shudders at this cry of anguish and calls each one to give a loving response of charity to his brother's cry for help" (*ibid*). One may read these specific recommendations of the Pope throughout the letter (pars. 1, 3, 5, 24, 47–48, 50, 61).

The kinds of aid which the Pope recommends are diverse and specific. He calls for taxes on the luxuries of the rich to be used in the "world fund" on behalf of the poor (par. 84). From the rich countries he asks for increased taxes to support foreign aid, more personal sacrifice on the part of the individuals in these countries, long-term, interest-free or low-interest loans, aid of technicians to these countries, stabilization of the price of basic commodities from the developing nations, planning and strong social governments in the developing countries themselves — all to be put into a world fund, preferably administered by an international agency of the U. N. (cf. pars. 33, 47, 51–52, 54, 59, 61, 78). The Pope is particularly worried about trade agreements, for herein lies the key to the future increased poverty or prosperity of the developing nations (pars. 56–61). He cuts right through the fictitious talk of "free enterprise" and "free market" between these two blocks of nations: "As a result, nations whose industrialization is limited are faced with serious difficulties when they have to rely on their plans for development. The poor nations remain ever poor while the rich ones become still richer" (par. 57). As an example of this, let us for a moment look at the example of Latin America.

To Americans, "our way" conjures up the attractive image of a great friendly power generously helping its poor neighbors. The Alliance for Progress, in a report issued in May, 1966, listed expenditures of $2.3 billion in the last five years. This amount provided the capital for 300,000 housing units; 22,400 kilometers of new and repaired roads; 1170 potable water systems; 1200 hospitals, health centers, and sanitary systems. It helped train

160,000 teachers, provided fourteen million textbooks, protected 100 million people from malaria.

Yet from another viewpoint, it must be realized that for the nineteen Latin American nations — excluding Cuba — the United States is the overriding and decisive factor in their existence. Every major decision they take, in domestic as well as foreign affairs, is related to decisions made in Washington. They are not, these nineteen republics, mindless robots, following the dictates of the U. S. State Department with cheery precision. They discuss, they dispute, they disagree. But in the final analysis they are being shaped into the U. S. mold, tailored to the pattern cut out by the United States.

It must be noted to begin with that aid by the Alliance for Progress is not a gift — except for a small part in technical aid and Food for Peace — but a loan. The $140 million that was scheduled as "aid" for Chile in 1967, for instance, breaks down into a $100 million loan, a $20 million sale of agricultural commodities (why this is called "aid" is not clear), and $3.5 million in technical assistance grants. The loans have low interest rates — often only one percent the first ten years and 2.5 percent thereafter — but they are not donations; they are to be repaid. Moreover, the recipient countries must meet certain conditions. All materials and equipment required for the various projects must be bought in the United States, even if they can be purchased for much less in Japan or England or elsewhere. Half of what is bought must be shipped in U. S. ships, at much higher rates than ships of other countries charge. If these additional costs, plus the relatively higher fees of U. S. construction firms are included, the "low" interest rates are no longer low.

There are other conditions. If any recipient government should expropriate an American corporation without what the United States considers "fair" payment, all loans are cancelled. The borrowing nation must accept Washington-approved plans for development and submit to stern supervision. The money is not deposited in the bank for the Latin nation; the government and

AID officials jointly work out a plan for that year's development. The plan must conform to AID'S ideas of "fiscal responsibility" and other criteria. Each project is then written up in minute detail — the road, for instance, will be so many kilometers long, use so many tons of cement, be completed at such and such a time, cost a specified sum of money. If the project is approved by Washington — which has the final say — the money is still not made available immediately. It waits until that Latin nation's businessmen import that much goods from the United States, and, with the dollars thus earned, the American government deposits the loan in an American bank, to be doled out in $5 million "slices" as used.

To put American aid in proper perspective, it must be considered in conjunction with two other phenomena, terms of trade and repatriation of profits. The United States gives Latin America in loans and grants about a half billion dollars a year. Another half billion, again in round figures, comes in loans from such agencies as the Export-Import Bank of the Intra-American Bank of Development. But both together — a billion dollars — are only half what private American entrepreneurs *take out* of Latin America each year. Adverse terms of trade, according to an estimate by a U. S. Embassy official, costs the nineteen republics a billion dollars a year, and the repatriation of profits drains away a similar sum (it was $11 billion for the decade from 1950 to 1960). Thus the U. S. public puts in $1 billion, mostly in loans, and private U. S. businessmen take out $2 billion in cash. These are not happy figures but they do illustrate what the Pope is talking about.

The last aspect of importance in the encyclical is Paragraph 37 dealing with birth control information. The Pope deals with the subject prudently but realistically. He recognizes that at the present juncture, increased population of the developing countries is eating up any savings which should go into expanded capital and industrial capacities. If one must build more schools, there cannot be more railroads or fertilizer plants. The problem is clear in such countries as India where each year there is an increase of some ten million to a people who already subsist on a near starvation level.

The Pope recognizes the rights of governments to do research in the field of birth control information as well as to aid in its distribution among its people. This is significant since most Catholics (and their bishops) have tended to deny this right to governments in general and in particular. Here is an evident example of that principle enunciated in the *Pastoral Constitution* of Vatican II: The Church must also learn from the world and to read therein the "Signs of the times" (par. 13). This is what the Pope humbly does here with no great fanfare. The stipulation that he does make is that such aid and information do not "check the demographic increase by means of radical measures" and that such measures "be in conformity with the moral law and that they respect the rightful freedom of married couples." As to what are "radical measures," it is safe to presume that the Pope has in mind such measures as infanticide, abortions and certain types of sterilization — at least that type that would be imposed by the state on particular couples for arbitrary reasons. Anything else as to what is against the moral law in matters of birth control is still under investigation by the Pope himself. Even in the case where certain types of birth prevention should eventually be termed as immoral by the Church, this still does not prevent government agencies from helping those couples — whose consciences allow it — to find and aid them in finding various and divergent methods of birth prevention. Outside of gross and evident violations of the moral law (infanticide and abortion) Catholics in the present difficult conditions of demographic increase have no obligation to press for such observance by governments (in the event of an evenutal decision on the part of the authority in the Church against the morality of one or another means of birth prevention).

Conclusion

To be a Christian is not purely to serve God but it is also a dynamic social ethic, a service to mankind; it is not merely a theology but also an anthropology. And although Christianity is directed to the "beyond," it nevertheless must influence our actions in the realm of the "here below" of fostering science and promoting civilization. It must give a deeper meaning to our bond with the world and with history. Solidarity with the agonies and problems of modern man, particularly and above all of the poor, becomes the sacrament of God's saving presence in the midst of the world: "I was naked and you clothed me; I was in prison and you came to me" (Mt 25:36–40). The social encyclicals of the Popes, John XXIII reminds us in *Mater et Magistra,* are nothing more than the continuity of this living voice of the Gospel applied to the modern agonies of men. The encyclical of Paul VI is a magnificent continuation of this living voice of Christ.

INDEX